GUILFORD COUNTY AND THE CIVIL WAR

CAROL MOORE

THE History PRESS

Published by The History Press
Charleston, SC 29403
www.historypress.net

First published 2015

Manufactured in the United States

ISBN 978.1.62619.849.4

Library of Congress Control Number: 2015932936

Notice: The information in this book is true and complete to the best of our knowledge. It is offered without guarantee on the part of the author or The History Press. The author and The History Press disclaim all liability in connection with the use of this book.

Contents

Acknowledgements

Generations of historians have made this book possible. Without their hard work and dedication to the history of our great country and the permanent recording of their research, very little would be known of the historic events of the past. This work contains multiple quotes, as it is felt there is no better record of the events of the past than directly from the participants themselves. Many of the quotes originated in the pages of the local newspaper, the *Greensborough Patriot*, which wrote:

> *The best history of the present war that has been, or ever will be, written is already penned. It will be found in the newspapers of the Confederacy. Any man who has a complete file of any good newspapers that has been published uninterruptedly during the war, has the best and most complete piece of property, which will serve to teach his children not only the great events that occurred in the programs of this unparalleled war, but to afford them a narrative more intensely interesting than any romance that was ever written.*[1]

The opportunity to author a book published by The History Press is greatly appreciated. To J. Banks Smither, commissioning editor; Darcy Mahan, production editor; and others who work at The History Press, thank you for the opportunity and assistance you have provided.

Thanks is extended to Jim Savage at Oak Ridge Military Academy for information and for introducing me to Marie Lowrey Armstrong Stewart, an outstanding historian who kindly assisted me with historical information pertaining to the Oak Ridge area and the Civil War era and who shared her family history with me. Thanks to the Gibsonville Museum and Historical Society for information regarding Gibsonville's history. Thank you to Sherry Boswell for assistance with photography and for being a great neighbor.

Thank you to Gwen Gosney Erickson, librarian and archivist of Friends Historical Collection at Guilford College, for your assistance with images. Thanks are extended to Jeff Miles, web content manager, and Sarah E. Koonts, state archivist, North Carolina Department of Cultural Resources, for assistance with images. To William "Bill" H. Brown, registrar, State Archives of North Carolina, thanks for your help in acquiring a map image.

Thank you to Jeffery Frank, Colonel John Sloan Camp 1290, Sons of the Confederate Veterans, for your assistance answering questions regarding Archdale, North Carolina. Thank you to Joanne Phipps Sharpe, president of Guilford Chapter 301, United Daughters of the Confederacy, and members of the chapter for your support. Thanks to Joyce Phillips, president of Mary Harper Morehead Chapter 11, North Carolina Society Order of Confederate Rose, for your support and kindness.

Family, friends and the four-legged members of my family have my love and gratitude always, especially my mother, Julianne Stamper Moore, who left the "head of the holler" with a strong work ethic and sheer will to succeed in life to become the greatest humanitarian I will ever know. To David Moore and Darlene Moore Ramey, I extend all my love and gratitude for all you have done for me. Samuel, for the historic journey back in time, I am thankful.

Introduction

Guilford County, located in the piedmont of North Carolina, was created from parts of Rowan and Orange Counties in 1771. Scotch-Irish, German and African Americans comprised some of the early settlers of the community once most of the Native Americans left the area. Religious freedom was one reason early settlers chose to call Guilford County home.

Guilford County consists of 658 square miles and is named for Francis North, First Earl of Guilford. Counties adjoining Guilford County are Randolph County, cut from Guilford in 1779; Rockingham County, established in 1785; Alamance County, established in 1849; Davidson County, adjoining Guilford County to the southwest; and Forsyth County, which borders Guilford on the western side.

March 15, 1781, is an important date in Guilford County's history as the result of a major battle of the American Revolution taking place at Guilford Courthouse at Martinsville, the first county seat. The British, commanded by General Charles Cornwallis, suffered severe losses after fighting troops commanded by General Nathanael Greene, resulting in the removal of British troops from Guilford County.

For generations after the Battle of Guilford Courthouse, people grew up hearing the stories of valor on the soil of old Guilford from their grandfathers and great-grandfathers and other residents, such as veteran William Cumming, who was held prisoner during the battle and enjoyed telling war stories to the children of the community. Cumming died in 1849, but not before many of the young men from Guilford County who fought for the Confederacy heard his tales. One must understand the mind-set of the Southern soldier of the American Revolution to fully understand the mind-set of those from Guilford County who served in the Confederacy during the War Between the States, the War of Northern Aggression, the Civil War, the War of the Rebellion or the Late Unpleasantness, as the war between brothers has been called. They were opposing an abusive government, in their opinion.

An anonymous author going only by "Athos" penned an article that to date is the best first-person account known of the events that unfolded in Guilford County during the turbulent moments of the war:

> *Whosoever lived in the South and yet fought against their State was regarded as a Tory and traitor by the Southern people as the Tories of the Revolution were so regarded by the patriots of those days. And if the South had been successful in its gigantic undertaking the so called* [sic] *loyal men of the South would have been held up to obloquy and disgrace for all generations to come as vile Tories and traitors to their country and friend in their time of trial.*[2]

Greensboro, named in honor of General Nathanael Greene, became the county seat in 1808 due to its central location in the county. The spelling has varied over time, and during the Civil War years, it was spelled Greensborough.

High Point derived its name because it was the highest point on the North Carolina Railroad between Charlotte and Goldsboro. The railroads played a significant role in Guilford County during the Civil War. High Point would later become Guilford County's second county seat. Upon completion, the North Carolina Railroad ran through High Point to Jamestown, five miles distant, and from Jamestown to Greensboro, a distance of ten miles. The next stop across Guilford County was eight miles to McLean's Station. From McLean's Station, the railroad traveled to Gibsonville, another seven miles, before exiting the county into Alamance County to the next stop at Company Shops (Burlington) seven miles away.[3]

Among communities in Guilford County today are Browns Summit, Gibsonville, Greensboro, Jamestown, High Point, Oak Ridge, Pleasant Garden, Sedalia, Stokesdale, Summerfield, McLeansville and Whitsett. Portions of Archdale, Burlington and Kernersville are also located in Guilford County.

Jamestown, named for James Mendenhall, was established in 1816 by the Quakers. Quakers played a significant role in Guilford County's history throughout its existence; the members stood steadfast in their beliefs during the turbulent war years between 1861 and 1865.

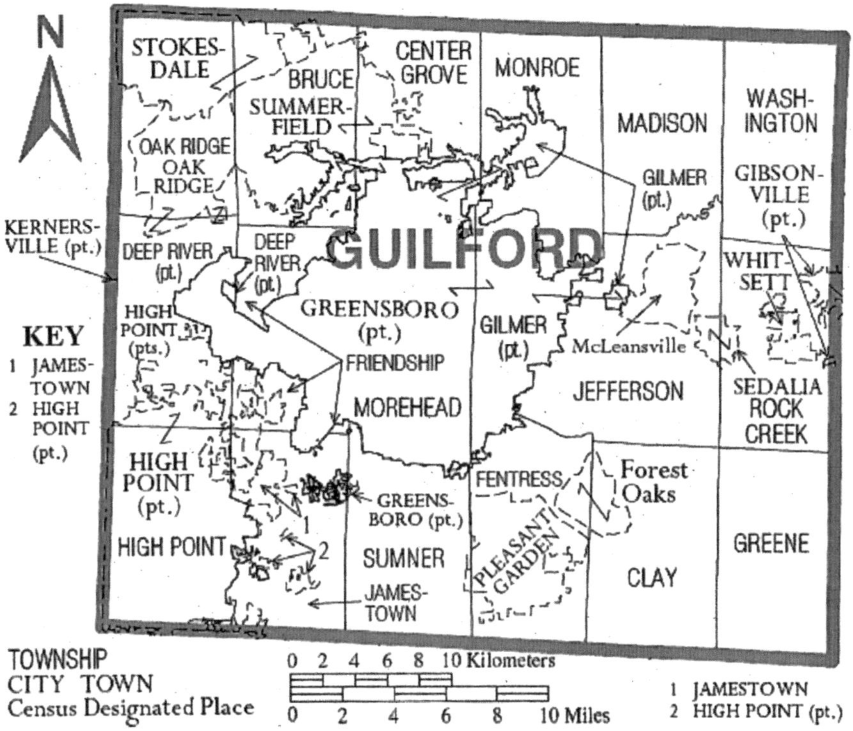

This map depicts townships in Guilford County, North Carolina. *United States census.*

Some of the community names have changed over time. Archdale was originally named Bush Hill. It was predominantly settled by Quakers, and today, portions of it exist in Randolph and Guilford Counties. Gibsonville, named in honor of Joseph Gibson, was called Gibson's Station in the years preceding the Civil War. During the war, McLeansville was known as McLean's Station.

Religious groups—first the Presbyterians, Quakers and Lutherans, followed by the Methodists and Baptists—were the first to establish churches. Life in early Guilford County centered on home and the church. Friedens Lutheran Church is located to the northwest of Gibsonville. The name means "peace" in German. The congregation arrived in 1740, established a building in 1745 and preceded the formation of Guilford County.

New Garden Friends Meeting, established by Quakers, has been in existence since 1754, while Alamance Presbyterian Church was established in 1764. Buffalo Presbyterian Church, established in 1756, was the mother church of First Presbyterian Church, established in 1824, and was located in Greensboro. The church was used as a military hospital during the final days of the war. Today, resting in historic churchyards and cemeteries throughout the county are the remains of many who once "wore the gray."

On the eve of a great war between brothers on American soil, many Southern towns created home guards or local militias. In 1860, the Guilford Grays (or Greys) formed in Greensboro for the protection of the community. They were young men, men of dreams and men full of youthful exuberance. They enjoyed the attention of the young ladies, practiced their drills to near perfection, participated in parades and memorial services and generally provided the community with splendid entertainment. War and its vile taste were given brief thought at this point in time.

Aggressive elements from both the North and South were agitating and soon would reach the point of splitting the United States apart, tearing apart the North and South as well as brothers and neighbors. Militias that organized throughout the South were supported by young ladies presenting banners and swords. The ladies were trying to encourage the male population to protect and defend their homes and the defenseless people of the community.

Guilford County was destined to play a large role in the war between the North and the South simply because of its connection to the railroad. John Motley Morehead, known as the father of the North Carolina Railroad, fought hard to have the railroad placed through Greensboro, the center of Guilford County, and his efforts met success in 1856. Morehead fought unsuccessfully for a railroad to link North Carolina with Danville, Virginia, until the demands of war finally deemed it a necessity, and the Piedmont Railroad, often called the Piedmont Road, was in operation in 1864. The gauges of the various railroads were not the same, and often the owners of the railroads refused to allow their stock on other railroads. As the war progressed, these situations caused great blockages of much-needed supplies from reaching the fighting soldiers on the front and caused great waste of provender along the railways of Greensboro, Jamestown and High Point, particularly.

In 1860, the population of Guilford County was slightly over 20,000. The population of High Point in 1860 was 525 people; Greensboro had 1,050 residents.[4] In 1862, as reported at the North Carolina State Convention, the population of Guilford County was nearly 16,000 whites, 693 colored and 3,625 slaves for a total of 30,956.[5]

In 1863, gold and silver watches and canes and pianos were some of the items taxed. Brandy was taxed at 10 percent per gallon, and there were

37,401 gallons produced. Other liquors were also taxed at 10 percent, which netted the county the largest return after real estate taxes. There were 1,127 whites counted at the polls and 30 free persons of color; all paid $1.20 on each poll.[6]

Over the course of time, many historians have tried to create an accurate rendition of the history of their ancestors. There are many stories within the story of Guilford County and the far-reaching consequences of the Civil War. The plight of the Quakers, the women on the homefront, the struggle of those in bondage, the fire-breathing secessionists, the abolitionists, the peacemakers, the carpetbaggers and the scalawags all have their positions in history, and their stories, in many cases, are yet to be told. The romantic days preceding the war and the patriotic first year of the war have captured the fancy of historians. The horrific chaos of the surrender of General Joseph E. Johnston's Army of Tennessee in April 1865 at Greensboro is an oft-mentioned event, but the middle years of the war—1862, 1863 and 1864—in Guilford County's history are dismissed with a simple myth: "not much happened here during the war." A great deal happened in Guilford County during those years and for decades following the end of the war.

Chapter 1

Before Disunion

Edgeworth Female Seminary, a beautiful setting for the education of young women, was the scene of a large May Day celebration on May 5, 1860. It was a very elaborate, patriotic and romantic event attended by many. A written record of the day titled "The Coronation" was published in the local newspaper, the *Greensborough (Greensboro) Patriot.* This is an oft-quoted article, as it truly captures the mind-set of the citizens of Guilford County in the year preceding the secession of North Carolina from the union of the United States.

The events of the day included crowning a May queen: Mary Harper Morehead, a daughter of James Turner Morehead and a niece of John Motley Morehead, a two-time governor of the state of North Carolina and founder of the school. The queen bestowed a flag, designed by the Weir family and manufactured in Philadelphia, to the Guilford Grays (Greys), a local militia company. At this time in history, militia companies were being formed throughout the South. On behalf of the students of Edgeworth Female Seminary, the queen expressed wishes that the flag would be a "Banner of Peace":

> *But we have placed upon it "the oak" fit emblem of the firm, heroic spirits over which it is to float. Strength, energy and decision mark the character of the sons of Guilford, whose noble sires have taught their sons to know but one fear—the fear of doing wrong. Proudly in the days past have the banners of our country waved o'er yon battlefield, where our fathers fought*

for freedom from a tyrant's power. This their motto, "Union is Strength," and we their daughters would have this our banner unfurled, only, in the same noble cause, and quaveringly through our soft Southern breezes, echo forth the same glorious theme, Union! Union![7]

Henry Clay Gorrell responded to the queen of May and aptly transmitted the feelings of the residents of Guilford County regarding the patriotic love of their country, the United States.

The Union, we trust is safe; our wrongs have been redressed; the bird of liberty once more spreads his broad pinions to the breeze which fans united North and South; and we are permitted to assemble here in peace with none to molest or make us afraid. Here, then, let us unfurl our Banner, as we swell the anthem, "Peace on earth, good will towards men." Ye gentle zephyrs as ye pass, catch the glowing theme and waft to the four corners of the globe—"Peace on earth, good will toward men." Ye delicate flowers as ye scatter broadcast your sweet perfume to gladden the heart of man, send with it also, "Peace on earth and good will toward men." And ye fair subjects of her Majesty when ye bid farewell to these classic haunts, and journey to the North, to the South, to the East, and to the West carry hence with you—the glad tidings of "Peace on earth, good will toward men."

The first sentence of the following verse is from the poem "Defence [*sic*] of Fort McHenry" by Francis Scott Key, better known as the "The Star-Spangled Banner," the national anthem of the United States. The remainder of the poem is the last stanza of "The American Flag" by Joseph Rodman Drake. Henry Clay Gorrell owned an extensive library, which probably assisted him with writing the banner acceptance speech:

"And thou star spangled banner long may you wave,
Over the land of the free, the home of the brave!"
Flag of the free hearts, hope and home;
By Angel hand to valor given;
The stars have lit the welkin dome,
And all the hues were born in Heaven,
Forever float that standard sheet,
Where berates the foe but falls before us;
With Freedom's soil beneath our feet,
And freedom's banner streaming o'er us

Gorrell continued:

> *Your majesty calls to remembrance, "the days of Auld land Sine* [sic]*," when the banners our country proudly and triumphantly waved over our own battlefield and when our Fathers on the soil of Old Guilford "Struck for the altars and their fires; Struck for the green graves of their sires—God and their native land!"*
>
> *Here, indeed, was fought the great battle of the South; here was decided the great struggle of the Revolution; here was achieved the great victory of American over British generalship; here was evidenced the great military talent and skill of Nathanael Greene, the blacksmith boy whose immortal name our town bears and to whose honored memory the sons and daughters of Guilford intend to erect a monument worthy his great name and fame.*
>
> *If any earthly pride be justifiable, are not the sons of Guilford entitled to entertain it? If any entitled to receive a banner of Peace who more deserving than the sons of those who fought and bled for and obtained that Peace which we have so long and so happily enjoyed; which we are now enjoying, and which we trust under Heaven, we ever shall enjoy. If any spot on earth be appropriate for the presentation of a banner of Peace, where will you find it? If it be not here, five miles from the Battlefield of Martinsville, here at Guilford Court House in the Borough of Nathanael Greene—here in the classic ground of old Edgeworth surrounded with beauty and intelligence—in the presence of our wives, our sisters and our sweethearts.*
>
> *And who more appropriately could present this banner than your Majesty, and her fair subjects? You are the daughters of Revolutionary mothers, to who we would render all honor due.*
>
> *They were help-meets indeed; many daring deeds and noble exploits were achieved by them, which a Cornwallis, a Greene, aye even a* [George] *Washington could not have done….*
>
> *They have passed from the earthly action, and while we pay to their memories the grateful tribute of a sigh, we would again express our thanks to their daughters for this beautiful banner, and as a token of our gratitude, we, the Guilford Grays, do, here beneath its sacred folds, pledge our lives, our fortunes, and our sacred honor, and for them to die. You represent different States of that Union which our ancestors established. You, the fair representatives of Peace, have come on a pilgrimage to that spot where the great conflict which gave us this Peace, was decided—to join with those to the "manor-born" in rendering honor to those whom you conceive honor is due. Most noble is your purpose, and most nobly have you accomplished it.*

In Union there is strength. This time-honored max has been fully tried, and has always proven true; but in no case has it been more happily verified than in the union of our Forefathers in their struggle for Independence, and in the union of these States…And we would have you remember that we are all in favor of union, union of States, union of hearts, union of hands; "union now and forever, one and inseparable."[8]

The election of President Abraham Lincoln in 1860 angered many Southerners. The residents of Guilford County watched and waited. Though he was not their choice for president, they stood steadfast to the United States hoping war could be averted.

The Religious Society of Friends found its beliefs challenged and challenging on the eve of the Civil War. Some of its beliefs regarding slavery and violence are quoted from a pamphlet printed in response to a yearly meeting held in 1822 at New Garden, *The Discipline of Friends, Revised and Approved by the Yearly Meeting, Held at New Garden, in Guilford County, North Carolina, from the 4th to the 7th of the 11th month, inclusive, 1822.* The pamphlet explained:

As a religious society, we have found it to be our indispensable duty, to declare to the world our belief of the repugnance of slavery to the Christian religion. It therefore remains to be our continued concern, to prohibit our members from holding in bondage our fellow man.

If any in membership with us, shall hire any in slavery, of their master or mistress, to assist them in their business, it is the judgment of the yearly meeting, that, in so doing, they promote the unrighteous traffic, and oppose our testimony against slavery if they cannot be prevailed upon to desist, monthly meetings are at liberty to disown them.

A proper regard to this testimony, would lead our members to avoid acting as executors or administrators to estates in which slaves are bequeathed, or being accessary to any step whereby their bondage may be prolonged.

If any of our members are concerned in selling or purchasing, or shall give away or transfer, any negro or slave, or accept any such gift or assignment, so as to prolong his or her slavery, or prevent such from the benefit of their labour [sic]*; they ought to speedily, to be treated with, in the spirit of love and wisdom, in order to convince them of the iniquity of their conduct; and if such Christian labour* [sic]*, they are not brought to such a sense of their injustice as to do whatever the monthly meeting shall judge to be necessary for the restoration of such slave to his or her natural liberty,*

> *and condemn their deviation from the laws of righteousness and equity, to the satisfaction of said meeting, such shall be disowned.*[9]

The pamphlet also shared the Friends' views on war:

> *Friends are exhorted faithfully to adhere to our testimony against wars and fighting, and in no way to unite with any in warlike measures, either offensive or defensive, or in carrying guns for defending their ships or persons; or privateering; or, as owners of ships, going with letters of marque—that by the inoffensiveness of our lives, we may convincingly demonstrate ourselves to be the real subjects of the Messiah's peaceful reign.*
>
> *And if any deviate from this our ancient testimony, or approve or show the least connivance at war, by attending at muster-fields or viewing military operations; or in any wise encouraging the unstable, deceitful spirit of party; illuminating their houses in token of rejoicing for victory obtained in war; or by joining political devices or associations; they are to be tenderly dealt with, and if they can—to be brought to acknowledge and forsake their error,* [or] *monthly meetings should disown them.*[10]

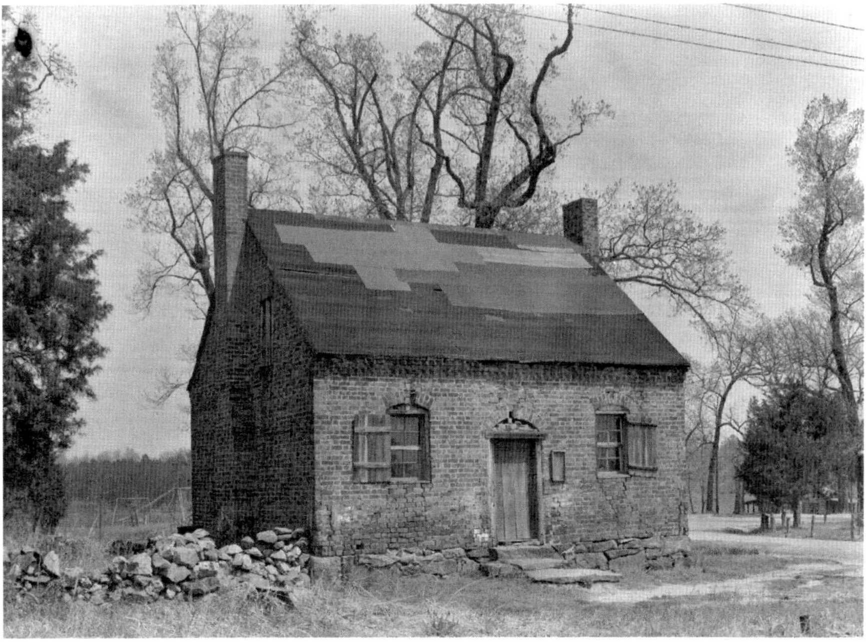

Religious Society of Friends (Quakers) members built several meetinghouses in Guilford County. Shown is a meetinghouse located in Jamestown, North Carolina. *Library of Congress.*

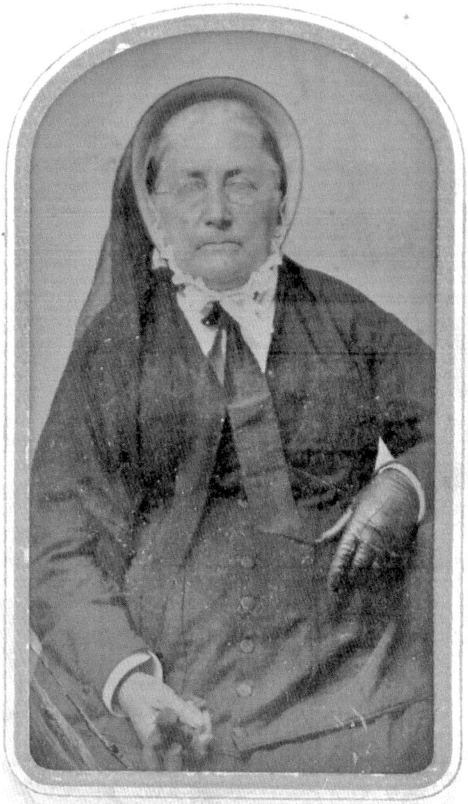

Delphina Mendenhall, a member of the Religious Society of Friends, worked diligently to emancipate those in bondage. *Courtesy of Friends Historical Collection, Guilford College, Greensboro, North Carolina.*

The Guilford County Slave Schedule of 1860 lists a slave owner, Delphina E. Gardner Mendenhall, widow of George C. Mendenhall, and states that she manumitted fifty of her slaves. Her husband, George, was previously married to Eliza Dunn, who inherited slaves through a previous marriage; upon Eliza's death, George inherited the slaves and was disowned by the Friends. George worked diligently to escort and settle slaves in Ohio before his untimely death in 1860 from drowning. After the death of Eliza, George married Delphina. Upon his death, Delphina inherited the slaves. Delphina attempted to carry out the orders of George's will that insisted on the eventual freedom of the slaves. Delphina was a Quaker minister and quite comfortable financially, as indicated in the 1860 census of Guilford County, and she worked diligently to free the enslaved.

The census record includes a vague description of the enslaved. The letter "M" is used to signify mulatto, and the letter "B" is used to signify black. Blacks would be considered darker-skinned individuals with ancestry originating in Africa. Mulattos were a blend of European and African American ancestry. Often the word mulatto didn't differentiate between Native American and African American. When a child was born, his or her freedom depended on his mother's status. If she were slave, then the child was also a slave, but if the woman was free, then her child was born free. Delphina's slaves were described as black or mulatto. Skin color was confusing and not a determination of slave or free status. Many slaves were light-skinned, with some described as having yellow skin color and light eyes of blue or gray. Some slaves were so light that it was possible for them to blend into society as people of European descent if they were fortunate enough to travel to non-slaveholding states and territories. There was another classification to describe free individuals other than white: free persons of color.

Mary Mendenhall Hobbs, a daughter of Nereus Mendenhall, wrote *Civil War and Reconstruction Through the Eyes of Mary Mendenhall Hobbs*, a collection of memories and experiences during the war years in Guilford County, which was published in *The Friend* in 1923. Mary relates an incident regarding her mother burning copies of Hinton Rowan Helper's book *The Impending Crisis of the South*. Mary's father was called to court in Greensboro to explain having copies of the banned book in his possession. He explained they were burned and he had neglected to read one beforehand.

One could be severely punished for having a copy of the banned book in one's possession. For example, Reverend Daniel Worth, a Wesleyan Methodist minister born in the Centre (Center) Quaker community of Guilford County, was accused of circulating Helper's book in 1859. Daniel Worth was born in the Center Quaker community of Guilford County on May 3, 1795, a son of Job and Rhoda Macy Worth. On December 22, 1859, Worth visited his relative Hiram Worth in Greensboro. At this time, aware of warrants against him, he requested the sheriff. Sheriff Boon took Worth to a frigid cell at the Greensboro jail. Worth's sermons were proven in court as incendiary in nature. In distributing Hinton Helper's book, he broke a law that was enacted in 1830 banning circulation of such material. If found guilty, the sentence was one year in jail and, perhaps, a whipping. If found guilty once more of the same offense, the penalty was death. Worth was found guilty and ordered whipped at the whipping post, but due to his age, the judge decided against the beating. Worth was sentenced to one year in prison. James Morehead and Ralph Gorrell defended Worth, while Levi M. Scott and James R. McLean represented the prosecution. All four men were from Guilford County. Worth was able to make bail and fled Guilford County to New York, hence avoiding the legal process.

In the years preceding the war, many Quakers left Guilford County and settled in western or Northern states in which slavery was illegal. During the war, the migration continued, and after the war, so many Quakers left Guilford County that it was feared the entire membership might leave.

The Quaker family of Levi and Prudence Coffin migrated westward to Indiana after having settled in New Garden (now a part of Greensboro), Guilford County. Their son, Levi (1789–1877), the reputed president of the

Underground Railroad, was born in Guilford County. He, too, would follow his parents in 1826 to Indiana. Prior to his departure, he was a member of the Manumission Society in Guilford County. In Wayne County, Indiana—which happened to be on a route of the Underground Railroad—Levi assisted fugitive slaves on their journeys to freedom. Levi's cousin Vestal Coffin is reputedly the creator of the Underground Railroad.

The Underground Railroad was very secretive. There were "conductors" who maintained the routes, "passengers" (slaves seeking freedom) and "depot stations" (safe places where the slaves could rest to gather strength to continue on their journeys). Though mysterious, it is known that the railroad had stations near New Garden Friends Meetinghouse and Boarding School, at Richard Mendenhall's Inn at Jamestown and at Joshua Stanley's house at Center. The routes the slaves traveled were marked at each fork in the path, usually by nails placed in trees and fence posts nearest the fork in the path they needed to travel. If the passengers needed to go right, then the nail was placed on the right side of the tree, for example. They traveled in secret at night, often following the North Star.

Chapter 2

War Begins

1861

The state of South Carolina severed relations with the United States on December 20, 1860, and many residents of Guilford County thought South Carolinians ruthless in their secession from the beloved United States—so much so that in January 1861, Guilford County voted overwhelmingly to remain in the Union. John Adams Gilmer (1805–1868), a son of Guilford County and a grandson of men who fought for the freedom of this country in the great American Revolution, frantically did all in his power to prevent war. He exchanged pleading letters with President Abraham Lincoln and wrote letters to over 100,000 North Carolinians in hopes of averting war.

John Adams Gilmer addressed the House of Representatives in Washington City (now Washington, D.C.) on January 26, 1861. He used his great oratory skills in hopes of avoiding war.

> *I tell gentlemen that if, in spite of all the efforts of wise and good men, the State from which I come from with this Government, my destinies are, and will be, with her. I know that when that event occurs peace cannot long continue. A war, a terrible war, will ensue. Whenever the people of the North and South have once appealed to the God of battles, for which I think with most fearful apprehension, a civil war will follow that will only end in the destruction of all the great interests of all the sections of the country. Whenever the event comes, I know my duty; and whether I have the nerve to be there myself or not, I know that such will be my duty, and it will also be my duty to devote to the service, any means, myself, and my children.*[11]

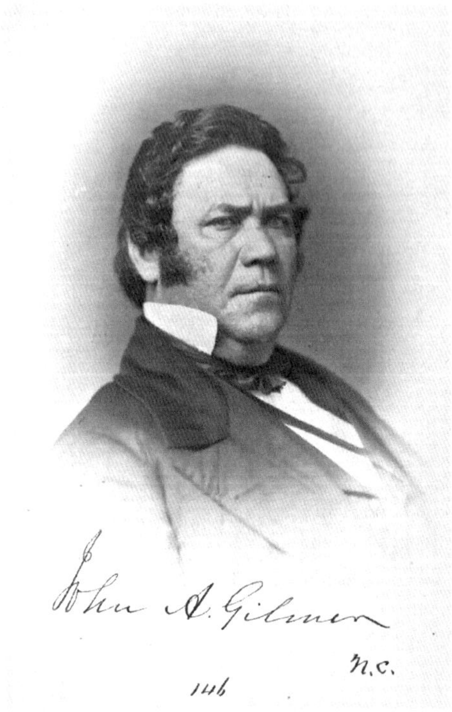

John Adams Gilmer, Congressional Representative, declined a cabinet post offered by United States President Lincoln. Later, he served in the Confederate Congress. *Library of Congress.*

Gilmer echoed the sentiment of many people in Guilford County and the entire South—their loyalties were to their native state foremost. Interestingly, so many comments in Gilmer's speeches and addresses came to pass that it is easy to believe he was gifted with a keen insight of the future. His only son to reach adulthood, John Alexander Gilmer, rose in rank to colonel of the Twenty-seventh North Carolina. As predicted, Gilmer's son risked life and limb for North Carolina and the Confederacy only to suffer and walk with a limp from war wounds the rest of his life.

The elder Gilmer warned:

> *I want gentleman North and South to mark my words: when these things come, when this bloody strife ensues, as it certainly will unless this spirit of disunion can be checked; when, mark you, this country shall be laid waste; when all our channels and communications of trade shall be broken up; when the shipping in our ports shall be destroyed; when our institutions of learning and religion shall wither away or be torn down; when your cities shall be given up for plunder and for slaughter; when your sons and my sons, your neighbors and my neighbors, shall be carried from this bloody field of strife; and our mothers, our sisters, our wives and our daughters, shall assemble around us, and, with weeping eyes and aching hearts, say: "Could not you have done something, could not you have said something that would have averted this dreadful calamity?"*[12]

President Abraham Lincoln and Confederate president Jefferson Davis shared the same birth state, Kentucky. Davis became provisional president of the Confederate States in February 1861. Davis was a former United States secretary of war and served in the Mexican-American War. He was installed as president of the Confederate States of America on February 22, 1862, and was president until captured in May 1865. President Lincoln was elected to a second term and assassinated shortly thereafter.

On April 12, 1861, General Pierre Gustave Toutant Beauregard ordered his troops to open fire on Fort Sumter in Charleston Harbor. President Abraham Lincoln requested troops to quell the rebellion, and Governor John Ellis of North Carolina responded promptly to the president that no troops would be forthcoming from North Carolina. As a result of the president's request, Governor Ellis ordered the Guilford Grays to report to Fort Macon promptly. The Guilford Grays left Greensboro via train on April 18, 1861. John Adams Gilmer, former United States representative and a Unionist, urged the Guilford Grays to go and defend North Carolina against enemy invasion, whether from the North or the South. Gilmer had much at stake publicly and privately as war rumors escalated. Gilmer exchanged many letters with President Abraham Lincoln in an effort to prevent war, and he also turned down a cabinet post offered by the president.

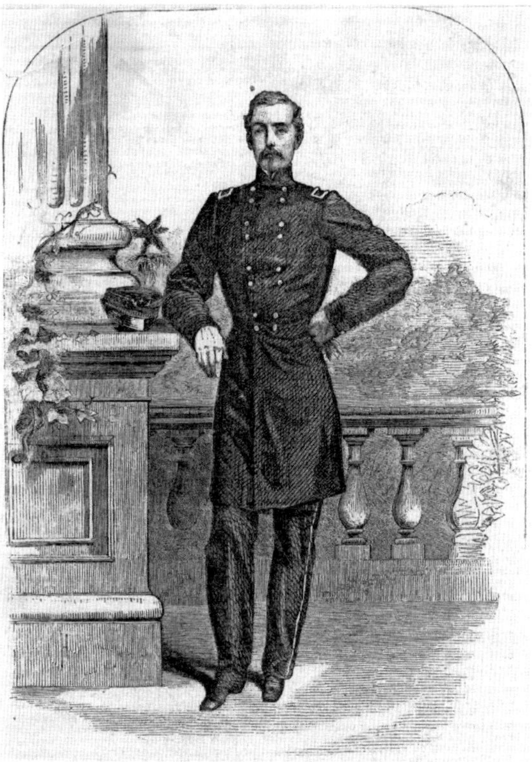

General Pierre Gustave Toutant Beauregard, involved in the war from its beginning, was in Guilford County at war's end in 1865. *Library of Congress.*

The Guilford Grays, established on January 9, 1860, enjoyed their days in peaceful pursuits, drilling, parading and participating in memorial services, such as the erection of a monument at Alamance

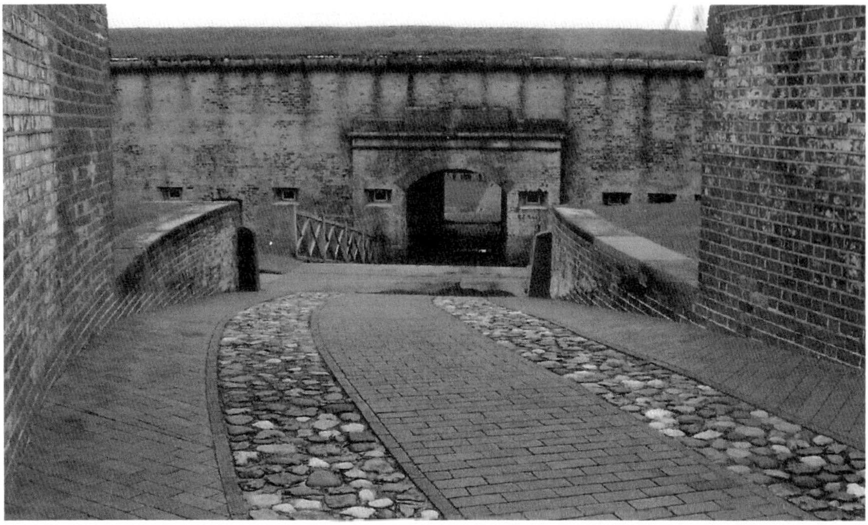

The Guilford Grays were ordered to Fort Macon on the coast of North Carolina, leaving Greensboro via train on April 18, 1861. *Author's collection.*

Presbyterian Church Cemetery in honor of Colonel Arthur Forbis, fatally wounded at the Battle of Guilford Court House on March 15, 1781. Many of the young men were away attending school at the time of the call to duty; many were disillusioned, thinking their duties would continue in a frolic, not yet perceiving war as a reality.

John Adams Gilmer and Robert P. Dick, Whig and Democrat, and Richard Sterling spoke to the citizens of Guilford County and the Guilford Grays before the Grays departed for Fort Macon in April 1861. The men echoed and endorsed the same sentiment: "Go! Defend your state! Carry with you the Stars and Stripes, and fight under that banner! Repel any armed force that puts foot on North Carolina soil—whether it come from South Carolina, Virginia, or Yankeedom!"[13]

According to James Reid Cole, who was on the scene at the time, Governor Ellis telegraphed Captain John Sloan (later colonel of Twenty-seventh North Carolina and uncle of Captain John Alexander Sloan) of the Guilford Grays ordering him to seize Fort Macon. The captain replied, "Under what flag?" Governor Ellis responded, "The State flag of North Carolina."[14]

Cole continued, "We couldn't under the United States flag capture a United States fort, for we expected to fight that flag; and we had not left the Union, so could not go under the Confederate flag, for that would be treason. So we lifted on high the Old State flag with its old pine tree and the serpent coiled about its roots and the words, 'Don't Tread on Me.'"[15]

Captain John A. Sloan, a member of the Guilford Grays, related, "On the next morning we saw floating from the flagstaff over the fort the Pine Tree flag, with the rattlesnake coiled around the base. This was the State flag. About ten days afterwards for some cause, and by what authority is not known, the State flag was pulled down and a Confederate flag run up in its place. North Carolina had not yet seceded, and this was looked upon as an unwarrantable assumption of command, and some of our company left for home, but returned when the State afterwards seceded."[16]

On May 20, 1861, North Carolina severed its relationship with the United States to become a part of the Confederate States of America. The Guilford Grays mustered into Confederate service on June 20, 1861, and sometime after that date became a part of the Twenty-seventh North Carolina, Company B. The Guilford Grays continued at Fort Macon, bathing in the coastal waters, walking the beaches, drilling and preparing for war. Each evening, Private Samuel P. Weir, acting chaplain, led the company in prayer, knowing death could be near. Disease was the first killer to afflict the company. Privates William Cook and George J. Sloan from Guilford County died from disease, the former at home and the latter at Fort Macon. The first battle the company participated in was at Newbern, North Carolina, on March 14, 1862. Private Samuel Hunter was struck by a shell fragment and died from the wound, the Guilford Grays' first battle casualty of many more. The Guilford Grays engaged in twenty battles, and on April 9, 1865, at Appomattox, Virginia, twelve of them were left to answer the final roll call.

The Twenty-second North Carolina, Company E (Guilford Men), was raised in Guilford County on May 23, 1861. Christopher Columbus Cole, born in Stokes County but a resident of Guilford County and editor of the *Greensborough Times*, rose in rank to lieutenant colonel and met death in battle at Chancellorsville, Virginia, on May 3, 1863.

Ads were increasingly published listing deserters, and in early 1863, the reward of $150 dollars was offered for several members of Company E. John Alred's name appeared in the January 8, 1863 edition of the *Greensborough Patriot*. Times were hard, and the reward offered was quite enticing to bounty hunters. The deserters hid in the woods during the day and pillaged for their needs at night. They often relied on family members to secret them food. Alred, a member of Company E, unfortunately didn't survive the war, as he was killed for the crime of desertion. Records were often insufficient, and some men listed as deserted were actually on

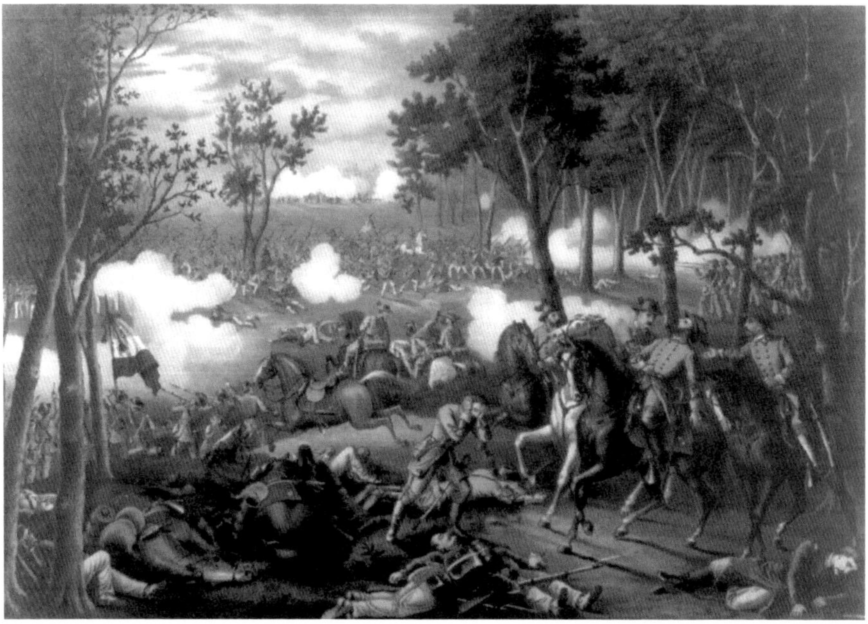

The Battle of Chancellorsville in 1863. *Library of Congress.*

furlough. Many farmers in the service of the Confederacy regularly shirked their military duty during planting and harvesting seasons, as there wasn't enough labor to do these tasks. Fears of their loved ones facing starvation was too much to bear.

William M. Irwin of Company E was captured after Gettysburg and imprisoned at Fort Delaware, Delaware; while there, he swore his loyalty to the United States and enlisted in the Third Maryland Cavalry, United States Army. Another member of the company, Christopher C. Perkins, was captured at Gettysburg, sent to Fort Delaware, took the Oath of Allegiance and enlisted in Company G, First Connecticut Calvary, United States Army. Thus it was a confusing time in the history of the great United States. People became confused in their allegiances and, in some cases, based their allegiance on their greatest chance of survival or attached their loyalty to the side with the greatest chance of supplying them with their next mouthful of food.

The Twenty-first North Carolina, Company M (Guilford Dixie Boys), organized on June 4, 1861, in Greensboro and began drilling at Camp Morehead (located in Guilford County) in preparation of being sent to Virginia. As the war progressed, many people feared there were so many

North Carolinians fighting in Virginia that it left coastal North Carolina ill prepared for the enemy; their fears became reality. Of interest on the roster of the Guilford Dixie Boys is William B. Hockett, a member of the Religious Society of Friends, whose beliefs did not allow him to engage in war. He was thirty-four years of age and was conscripted around July 1, 1863. By July 4, he was a prisoner of war and sent to Fort Delaware and held for three weeks. While there, he took the Oath of Allegiance to the United States.

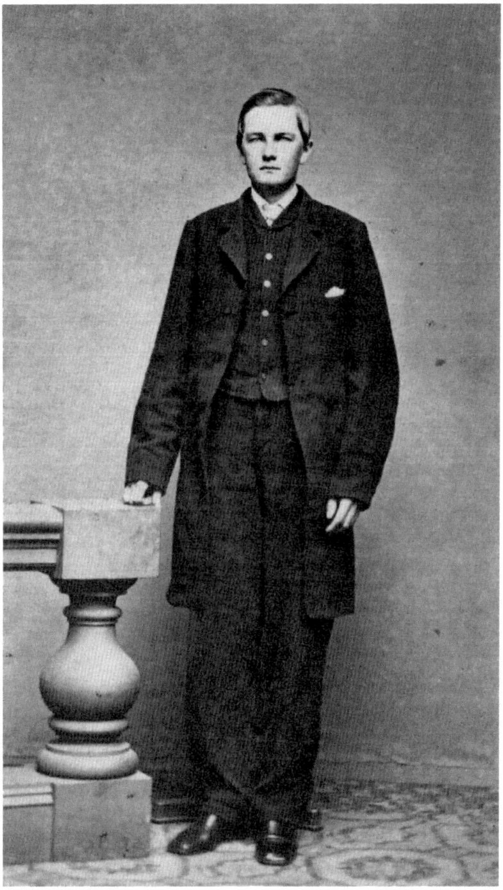

Quaker Tilghman Vestal was imprisoned after refusing to serve in the war. *Courtesy of Friends Historical Collection, Guilford College, Greensboro, North Carolina.*

Punishment could possibly mean death for the Quaker who refused to participate in the war. Tilghman R. Vestal was imprisoned for noncompliance, as he couldn't engage in war when required to do so due to his religious beliefs. He was taken to Castle Thunder, a prison in Richmond, Virginia, until eventually freed.

In view of the Quaker belief against war, the Confederate government felt it possible Quakers could assist in areas other than on the battlefield. They could help the sick and wounded soldiers in hospitals or supply food, for example. The conscripted Quakers could also pay a tax and avoid service in the military. Many Quakers refused to pay the tax because they felt the tax was for the benefit of the war effort; many simply could not afford the $500 tax. The Quakers felt that laboring in support areas benefitted the war effort and was against their beliefs also.

The war quickly reached all corners of Guilford County. Mrs. J. Sheck of Gibsonville, situated on both the Guilford and Alamance County lines, dedicated a poem to the Guilford Dixie Boys:

Our country is in danger
Of being invaded;
We call for our rangers
To come to our aid.
Come on, Come on!
Our brave Dixie Boys!
Old Abe Lincoln said
He would subjugate the South;
Go pour in your lead
From your great cannon's mouth.
Go, on, Go on!
Our brave Dixie Boys!
You are in a just cause,
And the Lord will defend;
The North has proved false,
They are not now our friends
Go on, Go on!
Our brave Dixie boys!
You go with our prayers
To meet the traitor's band,
Our eyes flow with tears,
As we press the parting hand.
Farewell! Farewell!
Our brave Dixie Boys![17]

The people of both the North and South often called upon their religious beliefs for support, and both sides felt their cause was just in the eyes of Providence. The citizens of Guilford County were equally exuberant that God was on their side in the mighty conflict.

On September 21, 1861, at Camp Fisher, a camp of instruction at High Point, the Twenty-eighth North Carolina organized. It consisted of men from various parts of North Carolina and a few from Virginia. At First Manassas (First Battle of Bull Run), Colonel Charles Fisher was killed in battle. He was highly thought of in Guilford County, and the camp was named in his honor. The Twenty-eighth North Carolina remained near High Point but a short time before receiving orders to proceed to Wilmington, North Carolina.

A large meeting of the ladies of Greensboro and surrounding areas occurred at Yates's Hall. Mrs. John Adams (Julia Paisley) Gilmer was called to the chair with Mrs. T. M. Jones, secretary. The group formed a Soldiers' Aid Society and divided Guilford County into districts. The district committees served as canteen workers, preparing and delivering food to the soldiers passing through on trains, served the sick and wounded soldiers food and carried them flowers to brighten their spirits.[18] The young girls and boys formed a Children's Soldiers' Aid Society. A little girl, Lizzie Lindsay, of the Children's Soldiers' Aid Society during the War Between the States, later in life served Guilford Chapter 301, United Daughters of the Confederacy, as president during the years 1913–27, and hers was the first signature on the charter list of the chapter when it formed. Lizzie Lindsay Chapter 776, Children of the Confederacy, was named in her honor and is an active chapter in Guilford County.

The ladies, true to their resolutions, created committees to meet the trains as they arrived in Greensboro. Early in the war, the ladies greeted new recruits and offered them food and drink as they passed through town on their journey to Virginia battlefields. As the war progressed, the ladies waited anxiously at the train depot for news of their loved ones on the war front. Heavy-hearted at times, with fear of each train's arrival and the news it might bring from the battlefields, the ladies met each train with a determination to meet the needs of the soldiers. Women in Greensboro served as surrogate mothers and sisters to the soldiers passing through Greensboro, all the while hoping that women in other locations might be serving their loved ones food and supplying shelter and compassionate care if needed.

From the onset of war until the surrender, notices appeared in the *Greensborough Patriot* detailing the work of the ladies. At one point, the Ladies' Aid Society of Greensboro sent twenty-four towels, eighteen feather pillows, thirteen shirts, eleven comforts, ten quilts, eight coverlids, seven pairs of drawers, six blankets and three boxes of lint to the Guilford Grays.

Wines, peach brandy, catsup, raspberry and strawberry acids, pepper vinegar, vinegar, pickles, essence of peppermint, honey, preserves, jellies, sweet and castor oils, tomatoes and peaches in cans, black and green teas, sugar, spice, sage, red pepper, mustard, dried fruits, tapioca, corn starch, arrow root, gum Arabic, mutton, suet, rice, red oak and slippery elm, barks, dittany, common and toilet soaps, teaspoons, cups and saucers, pitchers, mugs, crackers and sponge were received from the ladies for the hospital at Fort Macon.

Donations came from multiple sources in Guilford County, including donations from those enslaved. For example, Caroline, a servant of Colonel John Sloan, Twenty-seventh North Carolina, sent a jar of his favorite pickles. Knitting of socks and mittens was a constant occupation of the ladies and schoolgirls. A room was prepared where the women met daily to quilt and sew. Not a scrap of cloth was wasted; it was carded and made into bandages. Carpets were reworked to make blankets.

Thus the men, women and children of Guilford County primed their various talents in support of their state's needs and rights and, secondarily, their new country's needs.

Chapter 3

War Escalates

1862

War efforts increased greatly in 1862. The call for more men and more weapons of war created a whirlwind of action in Guilford County, and death and mourning escalated. Women's work increased as demands of tending the home hearth, the farmland and the children competed with the available time and resources they could commit to the war effort.

In 1862, the Conscription Act passed requiring all men between the ages of eighteen and thirty-five to enlist in the Confederate service for three years. The citizenry of Guilford County were upset with the Conscription Act, as most of their eligible young men had previously volunteered to serve. The names of those who had deserted were increasingly published in the newspaper.

President Jefferson Davis felt the railroad connection linking Greensboro and Danville, Virginia, was absolutely necessary for a successful military outcome. There was much politics involved in the railroad connection decision-making process and money to be made by entrepreneurs. Some people believed it would relieve the North Carolina Railroad of some of its cargo and thus decrease its income. There was also discussion regarding states' rights versus the Confederate government, which viewed the railroad as a military need. Other locations, such as Company Shops in Alamance County, were suggested routes directly linking the Piedmont Railroad with the North Carolina Railroad. A railroad running through a community, in time, could result in great prosperity, so there was much debate on the railway path. The railroad running through a community during war targeted the community as a place of interest to both the Northern and Southern armies.

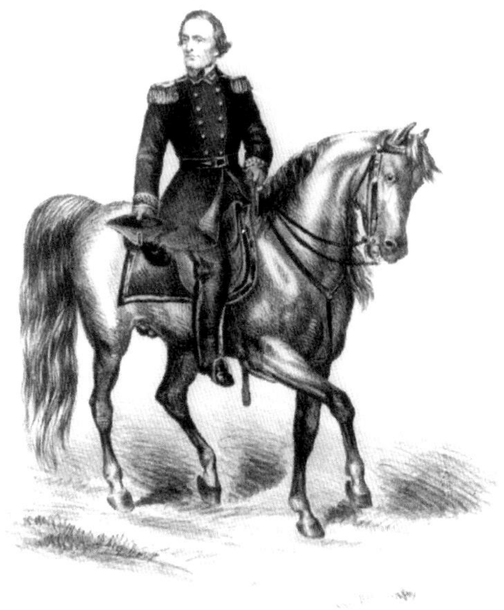

Jefferson Davis (shown here), president of the Confederate States of America, was born in Kentucky, as was President Abraham Lincoln, United States of America. *Library of Congress.*

An act to provide for connecting the Richmond and Danville Railroad and the North Carolina Railroads for military purposes was approved on February 10, 1862. Bonds in the amount of $1 million were appropriated.[19] John Adams Gilmer drew up the charter for the railroad to connect the North Carolina Road (railroad) to the Danville Road (railroad).

On February 8, 1862, at the North Carolina State Convention, Piedmont Railroad Company was incorporated. Jesse H. Lindsay, Ralph Gorrell and Levi M. Scott were appointed commissioners for Guilford County. W.F. Bowman in High Point and Jed H. Lindsay in Greensboro were to receive subscriptions. The secretary of war met with commissioners of the Piedmont Railroad Company at the Exchange and Ballard Hotel in Richmond, Virginia, on April 29, 1862. Among the resolutions, it was ordered that the chairman of the board call a meeting of stockholders in Greensboro once $100,000 of capitol stock in the Piedmont Railroad Company was sold.[20]

President Jefferson Davis addressed the Provisional Congress of the Confederate States, stating, "That certain appropriations, which otherwise could not be constitutionally made by the Confederate Government, come within the range of its powers, when absolutely necessary for the prosecution of the war, there is not doubt. It is equally clear, that when the military necessity ceases, the right to make such appropriations no longer exists."[21] It was felt the railroad linking Greensboro to Danville, Virginia, was a military necessity.

Slave laborers were immediately put to work at fifty cents a day to cut timber. A request was sent to the war refugees or anyone having slaves for hire to deliver the hands to the agents in Danville or Greensboro. Payment would be ten dollars a month, with owners providing clothing. Tools, building supplies and mules were needed immediately. Within days, the railroad agents were dealing with runaway slaves and having trouble securing the needed laborers.

There was such a demand for a new road for transporting military supplies that beloved General Lee was writing often, practically begging for work to proceed swiftly.

> *Headquarters of Army of Northern Virginia, October 25, 1862.*
> *Hon. George W. Randolph, Secretary of War*
> *October 25, 1862*
>
> *Sir,*
> *The completion of the Danville and Greensborough Railroad as speedily as possible is almost absolutely essential to us in the operations of the ensuing campaign. The enemy will, doubtless, make his attack in the present winter south of the James River, and will make strenuous efforts to cut off our communication with the South by obtaining possession of the Petersburg, Weldon, and Wilmington Railway. Should they succeed in this, hopeless disaster might ensue, unless we could rely on the interior connection, via Greensborough and Danville. This road should be pushed on to completion at once by every means in our power. I believe that I cannot urge its importance too strongly on the Government, and I therefore beg leave to call your attention to it.*
>
> *I have the honor to be, very respectfully, your obedient servant,*
> *R.E. Lee, General*[22]

Secretary of War George W. Randolph requested from Governor Zebulon Vance of North Carolina his aid in supplying enough hands to work the railroad. He desired 1,025 laborers and five hundred mules and a request to urge the planters of the eastern portion of the state to hire out their laborers.[23]

In February 1862, the Soldiers' Aid Society forwarded twelve bed ticks, thirteen feather pillows, twenty-four sheets, fifteen pillowcases, twelve comforts [*sic*], three pairs of drawers, five shirts, twenty-five pairs of socks, thirteen towels, thirteen bandages, one bag of raw cotton and one box of linen lint to Dr. James King Hall of Guilford County for the hospital of the Twenty-second North Carolina. The society's labors and generosity were not limited to those men serving from Guilford County but extended to all those in Confederate service. It is recorded that the Soldiers' Aid Society

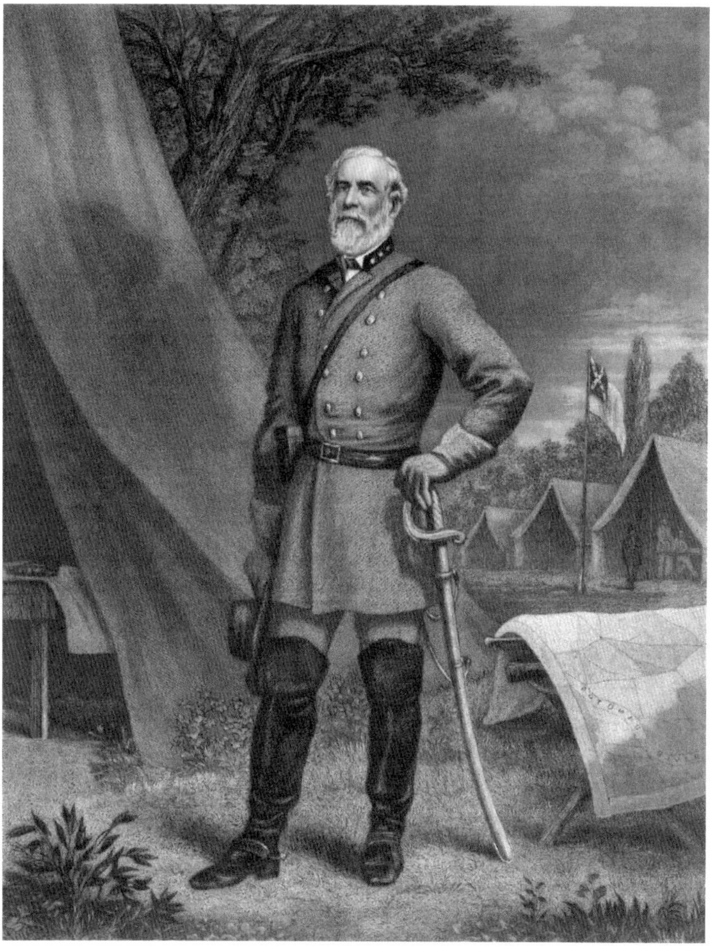

General Robert E. Lee, depicted in camp, formerly served in the United States Army before uniting with the Confederacy. *Library of Congress.*

of Greensboro sent shirts, sheets, towels, bandages, whiskey, blackberry wine, dried apples and peaches, sage, starch, eggs and soap to Wilson, North Carolina.

Sugar was furnished to the Ladies' Soldiers' Aid Society for making blackberry wine and cordials for the sick and wounded. Blackberries and dewberries were solicited from the country folk. Additionally, Mrs. James Long, Mrs. John Sloan, Mrs. D. Scott, Mrs. P. Adams, Letitia Walker, Mary Watson Smith, Mrs. E.P. Eckle, Mrs. C.N. McAdoo, Mrs. P. Doub, Mrs. R.P. Dick, Mrs. John Cole, Mrs. C.G. Yates, Mrs. W. Wharton, Miss M. Morehead, Mrs. J. Bethel, Mrs. R. McLean, Mrs. McCuloch, Mrs. James Dick, Mrs. Jesse H. Lindsay, Mrs. R. Gorrell, Mrs. Jordan, Mrs. T.M. Jones, Mrs. Alice Caldwell, Mrs. R. Lindsay, Mrs. Barringer, Mrs. Bumpas, Mrs.

R. Sterling, Mrs. O'Huber, Mrs. J.A. Gilmer, Miss Caldcleugh and Mrs. Spruce donated items. Ladies of nineteenth-century Guilford County rarely had their full names published in the newspapers, preferring to use their husbands' names. The men of Guilford County were frequently addressed with only initials for their first and middle names followed by their surname. Wives often addressed their husbands using "Mr." and his surname.

Items the ladies considered important to the troops included blackberry wine, blackberry vinegar, sage, red pepper, rice, sugar, canned tomatoes, ginger, nutmeg, allspice, tomato catsup, peach and blackberry preserves, pickles, butter, cordial, honey, bay rum, lemon syrup, corn starch, mutton suet, tea, cloves, blankets, mustard, brandied and canned peaches, scissors, dogwood and slippery elm barks, pennyroyal, dittany, socks, books and religious tracts.[24]

C.G. Yates provided forty pairs of socks. Samuel Curry (a person of color) donated a good hat.[25] Ladies of Summerfield in northern Guilford County provided shirts, drawers, pants, sheets, towels, bandages, soap, sage and mint. Ladies throughout Guilford County contributed to the war effort as citizen soldiers.

Trains arrived in Greensboro at all hours with passing soldiers. At times wounded soldiers remained and were nursed in Greensboro. A great curiosity led to many questions between the ladies and the passing soldiers, each seeking information about loved ones and home. Fear was constant with the ladies, and a fear of learning their loved one was among the injured or dead especially troubled their hearts. Medicine was scarce, and many soldiers had untreated wounds. Individual households were, at times, requested to house an injured soldier and nurse him back to health. General hospitals and wayside hospitals were established in Greensboro and High Point.

President Jefferson Davis requested that firearms be collected from citizens. There weren't enough guns to arm the soldiers defending the South from invasion. W.S. Ashe was in charge and had the authority to borrow, purchase or impress the guns if necessary.[26] The need for weapons was so dire that in April 1862 the First Presbyterian Church in Greensboro offered the church bell to the Confederate government. The bell was sent to Richmond, Virginia, to be melted down and reused to make weapons of war.[27]

The Forty-fifth North Carolina, Company B, was raised in Guilford County and mustered into service at Camp Mangum, near Raleigh, North Carolina, on April 9, 1862, with Charles E. Shober as captain. A son-in-law of John Adams Gilmer, Shober shortly became lieutenant colonel of the Second Battalion, North Carolina Infantry.

Also on April 9, the Forty-fifth North Carolina, Company C (Guilford Light Infantry), was raised in Guilford County and mustered for service at Camp Mangum. Companies B and C were heavily involved during the battle at Gettysburg, Pennsylvania, on July 1–3, 1863. Washington Brittain

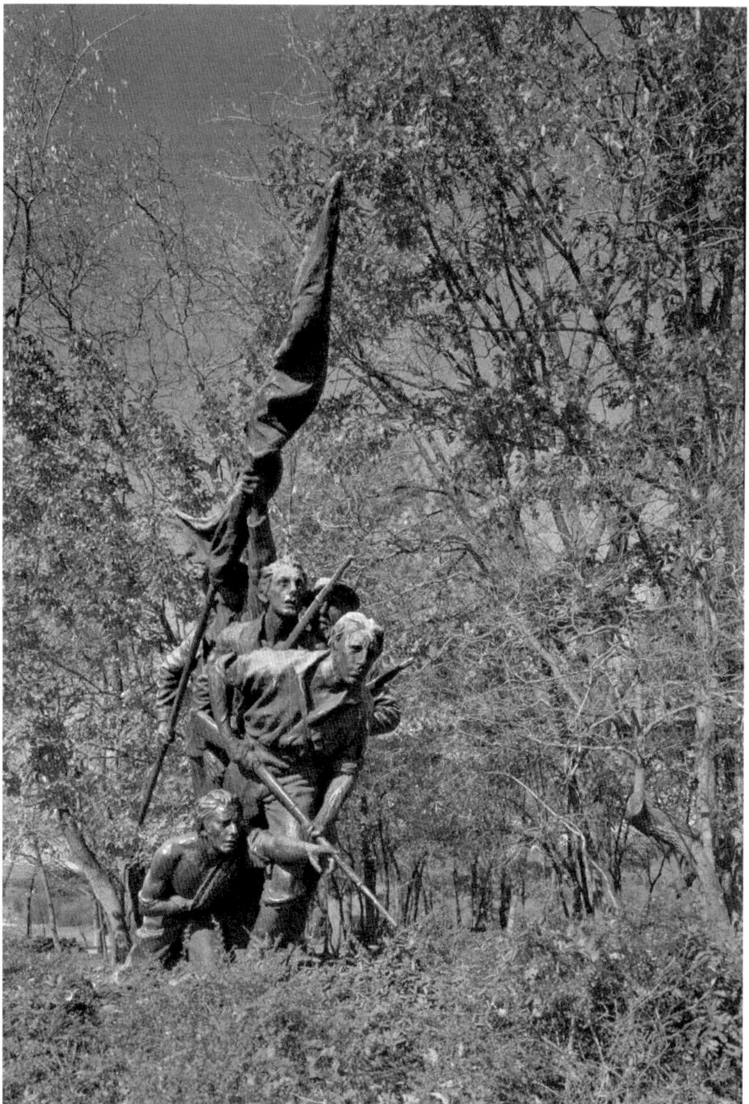

A North Carolina monument at Gettysburg, Pennsylvania, erected in honor of North Carolinians who fought there; many were sons of Guilford County. *Library of Congress.*

and Alexander Brown, Company B, were both killed on the first day of fighting. William D. Kirkman, Patrick Henry Lewis and John H. Pierce died of battle wounds. Many Guilford County soldiers were taken prisoner, and many were wounded. News of the horror at Gettysburg rippled throughout Guilford County. Sixteen-year-old Peter A. Wren, Company C, provided himself as a substitute for his father, James Wren, in 1863. The child soldier survived and was a part of General Lee's surrender at Appomattox, Virginia. On April 14, 1862, the "North State Boys" consisting of men from Guilford and the adjoining counties of Forsyth, Davidson and Rockingham became Company K, Forty-fifth North Carolina. Colonel John Henry Morehead, Forty-fifth North Carolina, was from Guilford County and did not survive the war, dying in 1863 of typhoid fever. His brother, Colonel James Turner Morehead, Fifty-third North Carolina, was wounded and captured at Gettysburg and survived the war.

Captain Alexander P. McDaniel advertised in the local paper for men to join his Guilford County company, which became Fifty-third North Carolina, Company A, on April 30, 1862. A number of men of Company D, Fifty-third North Carolina (Captain David Scott Jr.'s company), were gathered from Guilford County and sent into service on the same date as Company A.

The company of the "Stonewall Boys"—named in honor of Stonewall Jackson—was raised in Guilford County in early 1862 and mustered into Confederate service on May 27, 1862, at Camp Mangum as Company F, Fifty-fourth North Carolina. Thomas Jonathan Jackson received the nickname "Stonewall Jackson" at First Manassas and was much beloved by the troops. Generals Jackson and Lee were so beloved in Guilford County that a Lee/Jackson Banquet is held annually in Guilford County over a century and a half after their deaths.

Captain John E. Wharton's Company of Partisan Rangers, North Carolina Volunteers (Sixty-third North Carolina, Company I), and Captain Nat (Nathaniel) P. Rankin's Company of Partisan Rangers, North Carolina Volunteers (Sixty-third North Carolina, Company K), set up a camp in Guilford County in the summer of 1862. Once the companies were established and the necessary horses acquired, these two cavalry companies were to join ranks with Virginians, but the North Carolina troops objected, so instead they became members of Companies I and K, Sixty-third North Carolina Troops, also known as Fifth Regiment North Carolina Troops. Both of these companies had their origins in Guilford County but soon contained troops from many locations.

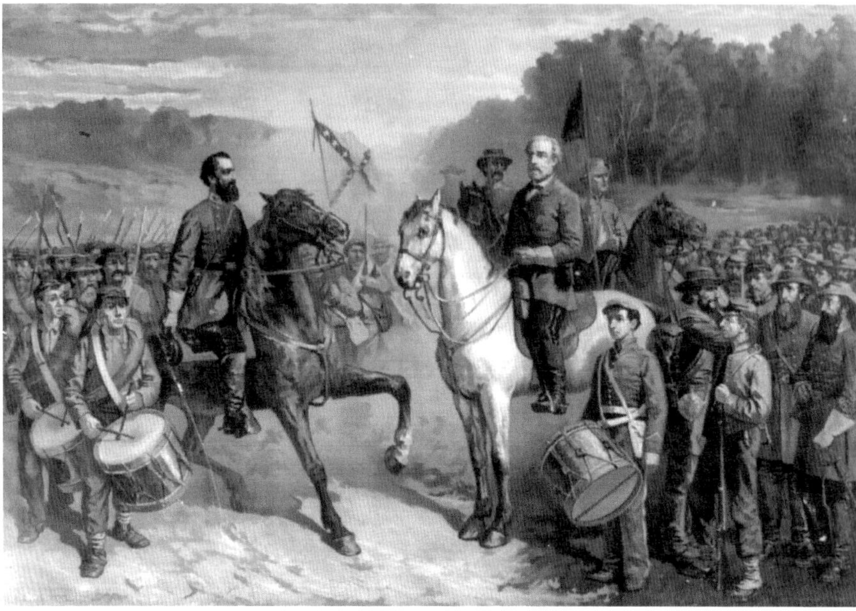

General Thomas Jonathan "Stonewall" Jackson, wounded fatally by friendly fire, met with General Robert E. Lee for the last time. *Library of Congress.*

Weapons, especially guns, were in high demand, and production in Guilford County increased greatly. The Quakers were long known as quality gun makers in Guilford County, though their intentions for the weapons did not include warfare. In early 1862, Clapp, Huffman & Company, located in eastern Guilford County and which employed foundry workers and machinists to produce farm equipment and parts preceding the war, signed a contract with North Carolina military authorities to produce sword bayonets and other items of military defense for the army.[28] This company became known as Cedar Hill Foundry and Machine Shop and was located four miles south of Gibsonville and eleven miles east of Greensboro.

The Tarpley breech-loading gun, invented by Jere H. Tarpley, was manufactured at Tarpley, Garrett & Company in Greensboro. The gun was tested at the armories in Richmond, Virginia, and Raleigh, North Carolina, and was patented by the Confederate States of America on February 14, 1863. The .52-caliber weapon had flaws, however, and only a few hundred were produced.

Cyrus P. Mendenhall, Ezekiel Jones and Grafton Gardner operated a gun factory in Jamestown. Weaponry was also produced in High Point.

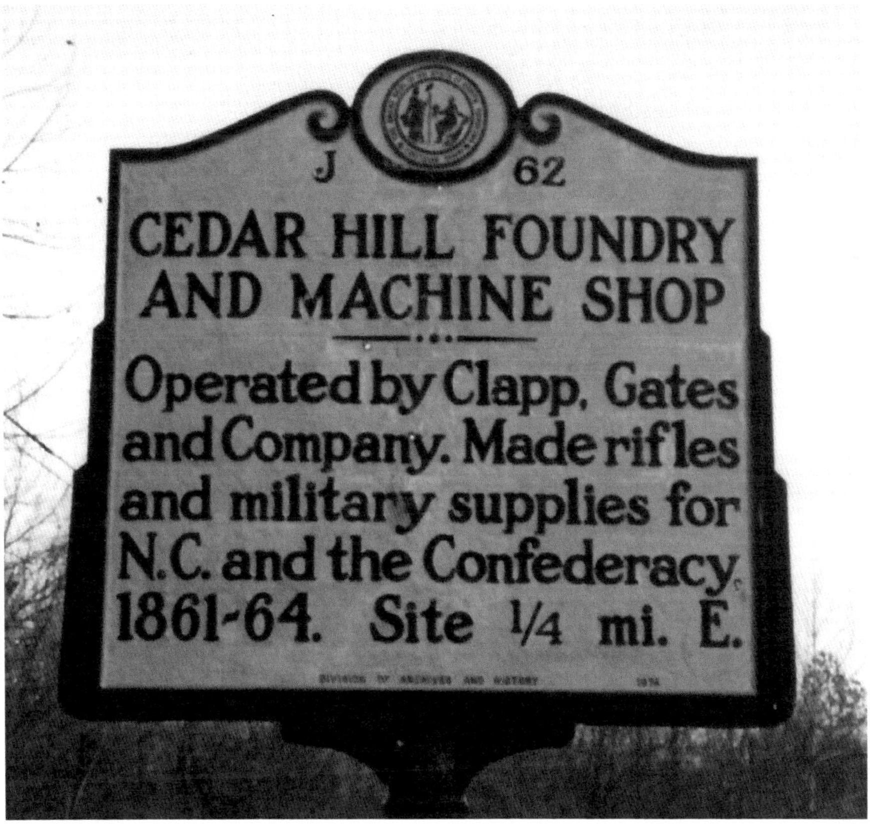

Cedar Hill Foundry and Machine Shop, located in eastern Guilford County, was destroyed by some of General Sherman's troops, according to local lore. *Author's collection.*

Richard Sterling (1812–1883), a native of Ireland, arrived in Greensboro to serve as principal of Edgeworth Female Seminary. Sterling and J.D. Campbell, a teacher at the seminary, wrote a series of textbooks, including *Our Own First Reader*, *Our Own Second Reader*, *Our Own Third Reader*, *Our Own Fourth Reader*, *Our Own Fifth Reader*, *Our Own Primer* and *Our Own Spelling Book*. The books were published by Sterling, Campbell and James W. Albright, who joined together and created the firm of Sterling, Campbell and Albright, Book Publishers and Printers.

The books were published during the war and for some time after the war in Greensboro and for the use of students throughout the South. The necessary stereotypes were brought by J.J. Ayers, who went to England and returned with them aboard the blockade-runner the *Advance*. The *Advance* was named in honor of Governor Zebulon Vance's wife. The firm also printed script for Greensborough Mutual Insurance and Trust Company. *Our First Reader* was copyrighted in 1862 by the Confederate States of America and was greeted enthusiastically. The sentiment at the time was that children of the South needed to read Southern schoolbooks.

Many Guilford County troops were stationed in and around Richmond, Virginia, prior to the Seven Days Battles, which occurred between June 25 and July 1, 1862. Many participated in those battles.

At the battle at Malvern Hill, the Guilford Grays, ordered to advance, faced a blaze of cannon and musket fire. In *Reminiscences of the Guilford Grays*, Captain John Alexander Sloan related that at the battle at Malvern Hill on July 1, 1862, "Parties from both armies, with lanterns and litters, wandered over the field seeking for the wounded, whose groans could not fail to move with pity the hearts of friends and foe."[29]

Soldiers from the county assisted in the bombardment of Harpers Ferry and were at the Battle of Sharpsburg (Antietam) on September 17, 1862. The Guilford Grays suffered the deaths of William Adams, James E. Edwards, A.F. Coble, James M. Edwards, R. Leyton Smith, R.L. Donnell, W.W. Underwood and William McFarland in that battle. The determination of the sons of Guilford County echoed with Captain William Adams's last words: "I am a dead man. Leave me and fight; let me die upon the field."[30] Adams's body

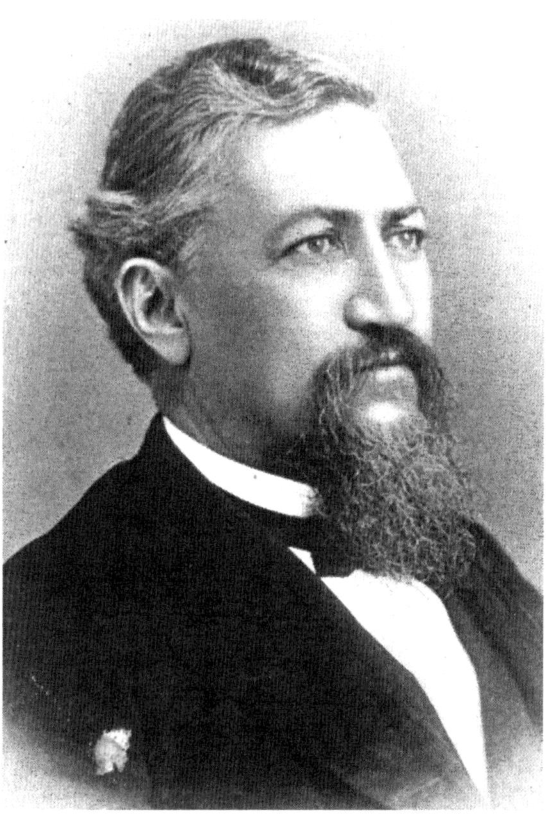

Colonel John Alexander Gilmer, Twenty-seventh North Carolina, walked with a limp the rest of his life as a result of war wounds. *Sallie Stockard.*

was eventually returned home and buried in the Methodist Cemetery. The Methodist Cemetery was later moved to Green Hill Cemetery.

At Fredericksburg, Virginia, on December 13, 1862, many sons of Guilford County were behind the stone wall bombarding the Federal troops commanded by General Ambrose Burnside as they attempted to ascend Marye's Heights. Second Lieutenant Samuel P. Weir, Forty-sixth North Carolina, Company F, was shot through the left temple while urging Colonel John Alexander Gilmer of the Twenty-seventh North Carolina, badly wounded in the leg, to leave the battlefield, and another son of Guilford County died horrifically. The friends and family of the deceased back in Greensboro heard of his death shortly after the battle; his body was retrieved and buried in Guilford soil in the First Presbyterian Church Cemetery in Greensboro.

The stories of heartbreak and sorrow of everyday people rarely survive the passage of time beyond a generation or two, but their stories should be heard, as they tell the history of their era as none other can. The Phibbs family, residents of Monroe Township in northern Guilford County and an ordinary farming family of the nineteenth century, gave their sons to the Southern cause. Samuel Phibbs, Forty-fifth North Carolina, Company H, died at his home on December 3, 1862, of a "disease of the lungs."[31] His body rests in the family cemetery. His brothers, Lorenzo and Robert, enlisted in the First North Carolina, Company A. Lorenzo died six days after Samuel at Charlottesville, Virginia, of pneumonia. Robert was captured at Spotsylvania, Virginia, on May 12, 1864, and eventually sent to Elmira, New York, where he died a prisoner of war on February 3, 1865.

An obituary in the *Greensborough Patriot* relates that Samuel left a wife and two children; Lorenzo left a wife and child.

> *Tis sad! They laid him in the grave,*
> *Far from his friends and home;*
> *And placed the turn upon his breast,*
> *Then left him there alone,*
> *Alone! Oh! No! One watched near;*
> *And guards his dust with sacred care.*

Chapter 4

War Is Hell

1863

The Emancipation Proclamation was enacted on January 1, 1863, by United States president Abraham Lincoln, freeing all those enslaved in the states he felt were in rebellion. It was of little consequence in Guilford County at this point in history.

Governor Vance of North Carolina proclaimed:

> *Whereas, it has been made known to me that a large number of soldiers from our army are absent from their colors without proper leave in this the hour of our greatest need, and it being confidently believed that a large majority of such, were impelled to this course by a natural and almost irresistible desire to see their homes and friends once more after so long an absence, and not because of a cowardly determination to leave their brave comrades to share all the dangers and hardships of the field alone…And let none excuse their desertion by declaring that they go home to take care of their families; they will add nothing to the comforts of their families by hiding like guilty men in the woods by day, and by plundering their neighbors by night; they only bring shame and suffering upon the heads of the innocent and their little children, when gray-headed old men, will have the finger of scorn pointed at them and the bitter taunt will ring in their ears, "your father skulked in the woods to keep from fighting for his country."*[32]

The powerful "shaming" of men shirking their duty was evident in the local newspaper at the same time ads were being published urging men to

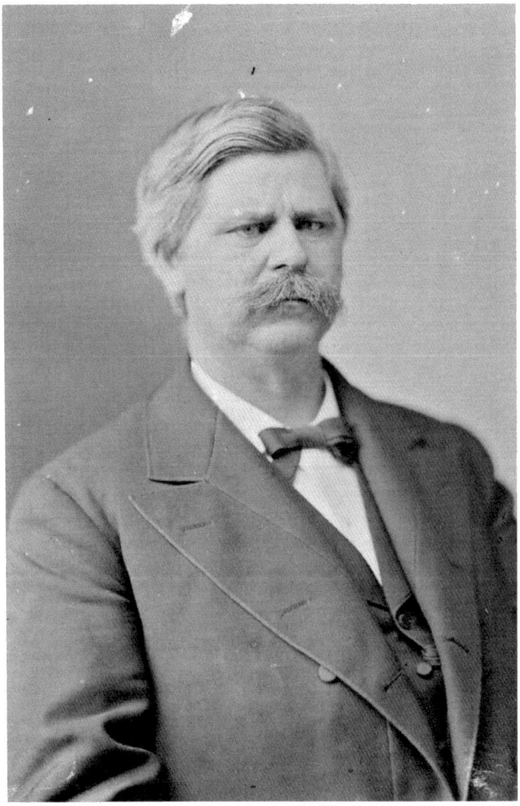

Zebulon Baird Vance, wartime governor of North Carolina, previously served as colonel of the Twenty-sixth North Carolina. *Library of Congress.*

come forward and enlist. The bounty to enlist at this time was $100, and the recruits wouldn't have to attend a camp of instruction but could proceed to the company of their choice. If absentees reported in a timely manner, they would receive a full pardon.

The publication of ads listing runaway slaves increased in the *Greensborough Patriot* throughout the year of 1863. Descriptions of the slaves and servants are of interest. Richard Beeson, of neighboring Forsyth County, advertised that his white bound boy ran away without cause. He described the lad as about fifteen years old, stout, standing five feet tall, with fair skin, light hair and blue eyes. Beeson offered a liberal reward and warned people not to protect or harbor the boy under penalty of law. J.J. Tinsley offered a reward of fifty dollars for his "negro boy Abner" if returned, or thirty dollars if put in jail. He is described as sixteen years of age, a bright mulatto with nearly straight hair. The owner felt Abner was passing himself as a white person. He was last seen in Danville, Virginia, leaving on a wagon going to Greensboro. M.W. Leach advertised for his Negro man, Sanford, age twenty-seven, dark yellow complexion, 140 pounds and about five feet, nine inches tall. Sanford could read and, according to the owner, would try to pass himself off as a white man; forty dollars reward was offered. A shocking ad placed by T.J. Motley regarding his runaway man, Dave—twenty years of age, black skin, heavy build, bought in Greensboro—remarked that his slave had many scars on his back and legs caused by dog bites and the lash.[33]

Female slaves also attempted to run away to freedom. An advertisement for Jane, twenty-two years old and heavy set, formerly owned by James Johnston of Alamance County, hints that she ran away to reunite with her mother. Jane's mother was owned by John Trelinge in Alamance County, and Jane's current owner, Mrs. S.B. Reig, felt Jane was probably in the same county.[34]

A slave named Charles—twenty-three years old; five feet, eleven inches tall; well built at 170 pounds; of a dark mulatto color and with a long beard—was hired out to work at High Point and Jamestown under the employment of Mendenhall, Jones and Gardner, gun manufacturers. Charles expressed an interest in running to the enemy. Albert Lomax of Summerfield offered a reward of ten dollars if Charles was captured and confined in any jail. Stories like Charles's grew more common as the war progressed.

The war effort demanded more laborers than Southern society had to offer, as all able-bodied men were needed to fight. Increasingly, slave owners hired their slaves to other parties and received pay from the employers for their slaves' labors. Many slaves were sent by their masters to Guilford County, especially from the eastern counties of North Carolina as it became occupied by the enemy, and the slave owners feared their slaves would be lost to them. Many slaves were brought from the larger slave populations of the Deep South to work because the resources of slaves, free persons of color, white males and white females were taxed beyond capacity in Guilford County. Many of the newspaper ads for runaways insinuated that the runaways left in an effort to return to their former homes and families. Often slaves were auctioned off at the courthouse in Greensboro. The death of a master often resulted in a slave sale.

Little is known of the slaves' feelings during this time, but some insight can be gleaned from the runaway ads in the newspaper. One ad tells the plight of Arthur. It was assumed he probably went to the Reedy Fork neighborhood, as he had a wife at Calvin Ozment's. Guilford County sheriff C.A. Boon requested Arthur be brought to him.

Women in slavery often endured the most horrid form of abuse. They had no rights to privacy and were subjected to any whim a master or a master's friends and kin might wish to inflict upon them. Often they or their children were separated forever on the auction block. Women in bondage in Guilford County in 1863 sold for extremely high prices—a thirty-five-year-old woman sold for $1,501; a girl, age eleven, sold for $2,400; another girl, age ten, sold for $2,105. For comparison, a horse sold for the average of $254. The possibility of being sold or a loved one being sold at public auction terrorized enslaved women and ripped their hearts apart when the auction block separated them from their babes.

Pregnant Prescilla, a mulatto bought in Wytheville, Virginia, and Gracey, a black woman bought in Farmville, Virginia, ran away from their owners in Jamestown, North Carolina. Prescilla was due to deliver her child at any moment.[35]

Enslaved women were not the only ones who suffered during the war years. Soldiers' wives received five to ten dollars a month to support their homes and families. Though the amount was probably sufficient at the beginning of the war, due to speculators and shortages, the prices increased as the war progressed.

Mothers, sisters and wives of the Confederate soldiers of Guilford County entered the unofficial ranks of a home guard on a mission to serve the needs of their husbands, sons and brothers called to military duty and to protect their children from starvation. In time, the dual goals often conflicted and overlapped. Additionally, the ladies vowed to administer comfort to all those serving in the Southern military with the compassion of sisters.

As the war continued, the women of Guilford County met with dire circumstances. Starvation was a real possibility, and their motherly instincts brought about a determination, no matter how horrid, to feed their families.

On April 8, 1863, Greensboro was raided by women. The *Greensborough Patriot* reported the event on April 16, 1863:

> *Early Wednesday morning a group of thirty to forty women were discovered a few miles west of Greensboro' heading to town for the purpose of breaking in to the stores to take whatever they desired. A few townspeople went out to find out what the women needed and if they were truly suffering with lack of necessities. As the women west of Greensboro were detained, a group of women arriving from the east of Greensboro, about twenty in number, armed with axes, hatchets, pistols, bowie knives, and sword canes battered through Mr. Willard's store door. The women were arrested with little resistance though one woman had a pistol aimed at a soldier; she didn't understand how to shoot it though. The women were placed in a jail lot, then the entrance of the jail, but were not locked up and guarded until assurances arrived that the ladies arriving from the west had been halted. The authorities guaranteed that the laws of the land must be obeyed.*[36]

Guilford County at this time was divided into eighteen districts with reliable citizens appointed to see to the needs of the destitute soldiers' families

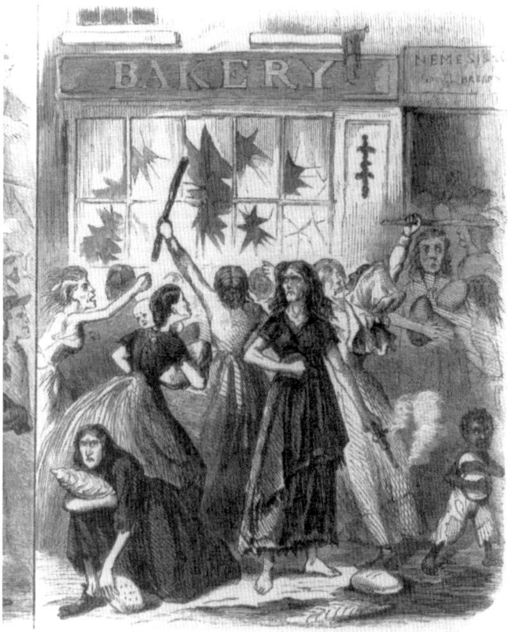

In 1863, Guilford County women united to impress food for their starving families. They were hungry, impoverished, in rags and desperate. *Library of Congress.*

to continue the work of benevolence and humanity. At the same time, men were withholding supplies from the markets in an effort to raise prices. Speculators bought up what provisions they could to control the price of provisions. It was felt that several persons throughout the county had a surplus and were selling their goods to speculators who raised the costs knowing there were neighbors among them suffering for the necessities of life. Such was the cause of the "mania" of female raids, according the authorities.[37]

Women wrote their husbands telling of the hardships faced at home, and as a result, many men left their posts to return home to help their families. Again, the local newspaper chastised the women pleading for their husbands' help, telling them publicly it was their duty to not worry their husbands but to present a cheerful outlook when writing them.[38]

Nancy Mangum of McLeansville in eastern Guilford County, a soldier's wife with six children, wrote Governor Vance a letter detailing the suffering. She said, "Poor women went to Greensborough yesterday for something to eat as we had not a mouthful of meet [*sic*] nor bread in my house what did they do but put us in gail [*sic*]."[39]

Mangum was quite bold, accusing well-known men in Guilford County and adjoining Alamance County of withholding much-needed provisions hoping to make more money instead of using it to assist the poor. She stated, "I have not got one sent [*sic*] of it yet since my husband has bin gon [*sic*] he has been gon most 2 years…We wemen [*sic*] will write for our husbands to come…home and help us they charge 11 per bunch for their thread and $2.50 for calico."[40]

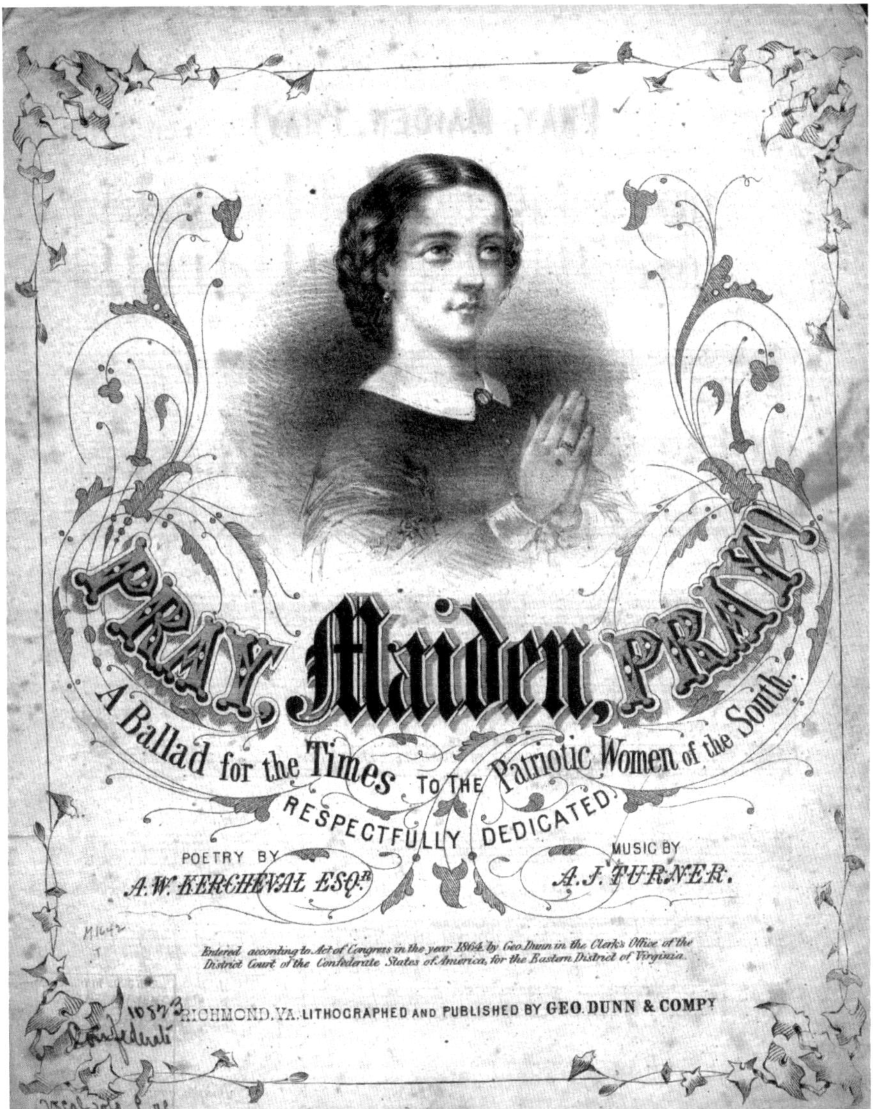

Women of Guilford County served on the home front in both traditional and nontraditional roles while their men were away at war. *Library of Congress.*

There is no indication Mangum's husband, Fielding, was absent from his post. He was paroled in Greensboro on May 8, 1865.

In June, while leading a charge at the Battle of Upperville on June 21, 1863, Peter G. Evans, Sixty-third North Carolina, was mortally wounded.

The *Greensborough Patriot* reported: "When the Yankees captured Col. Evans he begged that they would parole him and leave him at a house on the road until he got better; but they refused, saying that they would carry him to Washington if it killed him."[41]

Evans died in Washington, D.C., and was interred there in Rock Creek Graveyard. Later, his remains were removed to Greensboro and interred in First Presbyterian Church Cemetery. He was the husband of Anna Eliza Morehead, and thus she entered the ranks of the ever-growing number of widows in Guilford County. Widowed Anna Eliza was the daughter of John Motley Morehead, one of the richest men in Guilford County.

The battle at Gettysburg, Pennsylvania, on July 1–3, 1863, brought more news of death, pain and imprisonment to the citizens of Guilford County. Lieutenant Charles Webster Woollen died of disease in Richmond on July 4. Captain Samuel C. Rankin, injured and captured at Gettysburg, would spend the rest of the war at a Federal prison, Johnson's Island, in Sandusky, Ohio. All households in Guilford County were touched by the death thirst of the war. The Forty-fifth North Carolina, Companies B and C, were hit hard at Gettysburg. News arrived shortly that a dozen of them were dead and sixty-two were injured, several mortally. From the poor farmer's home to the mansion known as Blandwood, home of the

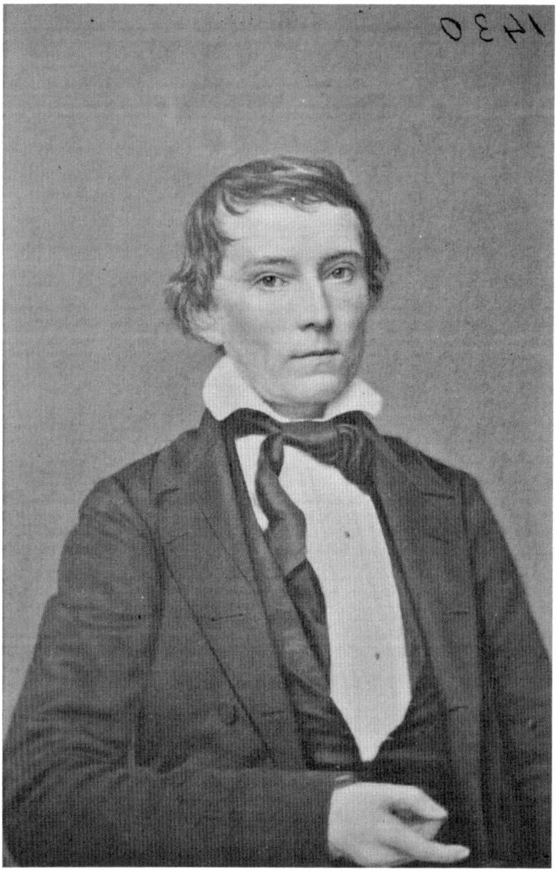

Confederate vice president Alexander Hamilton Stephens passed through Guilford County in 1863 and stayed at the home of Jesse Lindsay. *Library of Congress.*

Moreheads, war's evil touched all. Sergeant Alphonzo G. Causey, of Guilford County, was wounded severely in the arm on July 1, but he continued his duties "until the last gun was fired and all the prisoners secured, before he went to the hospital…there is no braver more noble and patriotic man living."[42] Causey survived Gettysburg but not the war and died in battle the following year.

In July 1863, the people of Guilford County were witness to Confederate vice president Alexander Stephens traveling from Danville, Virginia, in a buggy practically unattended. Jesse H. Lindsay offered his home in Greensboro as shelter to Stephens, and a huge crowd gathered and urged the vice president to speak. Stephens kindly thanked them "for the mark of respect thus shown him" and went over current events and expressed his confidence in a positive outcome to the war. The Greensboro brass band provided the entertainment.[43]

Newspapers increasingly published articles relating to the peace movement in both the North and South. Many of the articles were published with aliases. The soldiers of the South, in return, published articles deploring the peace movement. The Twenty-seventh North Carolina published a notice:

> *Whereas, we, the officers and soldiers of the 27th North Carolina regiment have heard with mingled shame and indignation, of the existence in our dear old North State of a feeling of discouragement on the part of a few who have never known the impulses of true soldiers at the recent reverse to our glorious cause, which feeling, unless immediately checked, will serve but to discourage our brave men, now so cheerfully struggling for the establishment of our independence; to raise the hopes of our wicked, though disheartened foe, and to disgrace the name of the beloved North Carolina; and whereas, that unprincipled and weather-cock sheet, the North Carolina Standard has constituted itself the exponent of these prejudicial views, and has been laboring assiduously to establish a submission party, by advocating the offer of term to the enemy; Therefore be it resolved 1st, That after two years and a half of service in the defense of the Southern cause although earnestly desiring the return of peace and its incident joys and prosperity, we still cannot and will not assent to any peace other than that established on our unqualified and perpetual separation from the Northern States, and the sure and complete independence of the Southern Confederacy. That peace upon any other terms, and especially upon these which, we fear, would satisfy the croaking spirits at home, of whom the editor of the North Carolina Standard is chief, would be an insult to our*

> *noble, and lamented dead, as well as a shameful sacrifice of our purpose, our patriotism, and our courage.*
>
> *Resolved 2nd, That we can see no cause whatever of despondency or apprehension, and we feel confident, that the assistance of our friends at home, both male and female, in encouraging a full and unhesitating response to the late extension of the conscription act, and the eloquent appeal of our excellent President, and the earnest and noble efforts of our beloved Governor, we shall soon be more than superior to our insolent foe, and before the expiration of another twelve months, will dictate peace to him upon our own honorable terms...Captain John A. Sloan, James R. Pierce of Guilford County witnessed the resolutions.*[44]

The Confederate Congress had the power to order men to serve in the military of the Confederacy. In an attempt to fill the depleted ranks, the age requirements for military service consistently increased as the war progressed. An act was approved on September 27, 1862, by the Confederate Congress to increase the age limit to forty-five. Confederate president Jefferson Davis proclaimed:

> *Now, therefore, I, Jefferson Davis, President of the Confederate States of America, do by virtue of the powers vested in me as aforesaid, call out and place in the military service of the Confederate States, all white men residents of said States between the ages of eighteen and forty-five, not legally exempted from military service, and I do hereby order and direct that all persons subject to this call and not now in the military service, do upon being enrolled, forthwith repair to the conscript camps established in the respective States of which they may be residents, under pain of being held and punished as deserters in the event of their failure to obey this call as provided in said laws. And I do further order and direct, that the enrolling officers of the several States proceed at once to enroll all persons embraced within the terms of this proclamation and not heretofore enrolled. And I do further order, that it shall be lawful for any person embraced within this call to volunteer for service before enrollment, and that persons so volunteering be allowed to select the arm of service and the company which they desire to join, provided such company be deficient in the full number of men allowed by law for its organization. Given under my hand, and the Seal of the Confederate States of America, at the city of Richmond, this fifteenth day of July in the year of our Lord one thousand eight hundred and sixty three.*[45]

On August 24, 1863, John Adams Gilmer, of Guilford County and a candidate for Confederate congress from the Sixth Congressional District, advocated a continuance of the war and a peace acceptance on no terms other than permanent separation from the United States and an acknowledgement of Confederate independence.

The people of Guilford County met at the courthouse in Greensboro on September 5, 1863, "in order to give expression to their views and opinions on public affairs at this momentous period in the history of our country."[46] Peter Adams, who suffered the loss of a son on the battlefield of Sharpsburg, was called to chair. A committee of ten was established; Ralph Gorrell spoke on behalf of the committee.

> *We are in the midst of a revolution in which our lives, our liberty and our property are placed in the most imminent peril; and whereas an unjust and bloody war is waged against us by our enemies for no other reason that we refuse to be their slaves—a war unparalleled in the history of the civilized nations for its cruelty and ferocity, and which has been seldom equaled, in its atrocity in the annals of slaves and barbarians; and whereas, this unrighteous war is waged against us by the existing government of the United States with the avowed purpose of reducing the people of these Confederate States to subjugation and ruin the most abject and overwhelming, they refusing even to listen to any terms to mitigate the horrors of the strife which they are waging, and to put it upon the well-established principle of civilized warfare; and whereas, we most bitterly deplore the continuance of the bloody strife, and desire that its horrors should be brought to a speedy termination; Therefore Resolved, That we earnestly desire that this cruel and bloody war in which we are engaged, may be brought to a speedy close; the lives of our brave soldiers may be preserved, and that peace with all its blessings may again smile upon our land; but we can be satisfied with no peace established upon any basis short of the acknowledgement and independence of the Confederate States; and we most earnestly recommend to our authorities to embrace every opportunity for negotiating with our enemies for peace upon the basis of entire separation and independence, whenever they shall manifest any disposition whatever to treat on that subject. Resolved. That we the people of Guilford have unabated confidence in the justice of our cause, and that, relying upon the protection and favor of divine Providence, we will continue to sustain it will all the means in our power against our cruel, relentless and blood thirsty* [sic] *enemies. Resolved, that our soldiers in the field, in all their peril, trials, privations*

> *and self-denials, have our warmest sympathies and thanks; that the valor and prowess exhibited by them in defending our country's rights, have appalled their enemies, surprised the world, and commit them to our highest consideration and gratitude. They have acquitted themselves like heroes determined to be free, and have covered themselves with undying honor and fame. Resolved, that we have full confidence in the political integrity and patriotism of President Davis and Governor Vance, and we pledge to their respective administrations our cordial support and co-operation* [sic] *in the cause in which our country is now engaged.*[47]

Meanwhile, newspapers were filled with death announcements, and the call for peace grew louder in both the North and the South. The emotional expense of the war was inconceivable. Memorials in the form of poems, respect memorials and remembrances detail the suffering in camp and at home. Joseph W. Rankin died from wounds received in battle at Bristow Station. A poem in memory of Rankin was published in the *Greensborough Patriot.* The author signed the poem using his initials, J.J.T.:

> *My best beloved friend is gone.*
> *And now how wrenched is my fate*
> *Without him, desolate, alone,*
> *I loved him with a brother's love,*
> *I love him like a brother still.*
> *For he's not dead, but gone above…*
> *The Word of God was his delight,*
> *Best treasure of the pure and good*
> *He ever bore it near his heart.*
> *And left it crimsoned with his blood.*
> *This blest memorial he sends,*
> *With blood marks on the pages worn*
> *To point the hopes of weeping friends*
> *To that blest land where he is gone*
> *And now with faith and hope and trust.*
> *We pass upon life's stormy sea.*[48]

The dying Rankin's plea was that his Bible, covered in his blood and fingerprints, be delivered to his father.

At the battle at Bristow Station on October 14, 1863, the Guilford Grays were nearly obliterated. Sergeant Major Robert Dudley Weatherly, fatally shot by a bullet that passed through his body and struck Colonel John Alexander Gilmer, was taken by wagon ambulance to Richmond. His parents, from Guilford County, reached him before his death and after death brought his body home to be buried in Guilford soil.[49]

Tragedies occurred at home also. Lieutenant Paris Chipman Stuart was guarding the Jamestown railroad bridge on July 8, 1863, when he fell asleep on the track and was killed.[50]

In 1863, exemptions from the military in District Six (of which Guilford County is a part) included individuals working at the asylum, apothecaries, blacksmiths, county and state officers, soldiers on detail, disabled individuals, factory workers, those working in foundries, militia officers, magistrates, millwrights, mail carriers, miners, overseers, preachers, shoemakers, saddle makers, schoolteachers, tanners, telegraph operators, wagon makers and government agents for a total 4,554 exemptions. Included in the count are 41 noncombatants (probably religious based) and 8 foreigners. There were 363 men conscripted for service in the Confederate States military, and 748 men were already in the ranks serving as substitutes. Exempted railroad employees numbered 200.

Exemptions were not accepted based on one's religious beliefs. Quakers understood the pressure of the current situation, and though they may have felt a sense of duty to their government, it was more important to remember no human-imposed obligation overrides the obedience to God's commands. The *Greensborough Patriot* reported on a meeting of English Quakers held in London, England, regarding their concerns about the war in America and its effect on Quakers and all Christians: "And let us remember that the peaceable principles of the Gospel will ever prevail in the governments of nations in proportion as the influence of these principles is felt and exhibited in the hearts and lives of the individual citizens."[51]

The Southern Quakers were cut off from their Northern and foreign counterparts due to the war. The war had a profound effect on other religions and resulted in some churches splitting apart along the same boundaries as the North and the South.

Not only religious groups but also foreign governments watched the events unfold in the War Between the States in America. The Confederacy hoped to garner foreign support in its war effort because the Confederate States, with limited resources, were engaged in battle with a country that enjoyed virtually unlimited resources and a constant supply of immigrants to fill depleted military ranks. The United States enjoyed foreign recognition as a country, while the Confederate States struggled for foreign recognition as an independent country. If the Confederate States could be recognized by foreign governments as an independent nation, trade could resume and supply the needs of the citizens and the Confederate army. Instead, the Confederacy had to rely on blockade runners to meet the need for foreign goods. The blockade runners were not always successful, and supplies were not consistent. As the war progressed, the sons of Guilford County serving in the Confederate army suffered for lack of supplies, which outraged their loved ones.

In late 1863, the Guilford Men were without clothing, some without shoes, and were in dire need of under clothing and socks, according to the local newspaper, which wrote, "If the government cannot or will not clothe these men let their friends at home see to it at once they are provided for. There are no soldiers in the Confederate Army more deserving than the 'Guilford Men.'"[52]

The Twenty-first North Carolina in late 1863 was on detached service in the Guilford County area and in November was ordered to "report at Richmond, and the whole regiment take the trains at High Point." The Alamance Church prepared the soldiers a dinner in gratitude a week or so before they left.[53] The patriotic people of Guilford County honored and attempted to serve the sons of Guilford a taste of home when their regiments were encamped in or passing through the county.

The emotional impact on the citizens of Guilford County was overwhelming, and those feelings were often vented by writing diaries, poetry and memorials in an attempt to verbalize the internal strife that the war, with all its heartache and hell, imposed on the very core of their being. A poem memorializing the death of eighteen-year-old John Frazier, Twenty-second North Carolina, Company E, highlighted the fact the citizens of Guilford felt no one was more important than those such as this teenage farmer of Guilford County and those like him who suffered and died in the defense of his country.

Old Guilford was his native home,
The place he loved so well,
Amid her streams and vales alone
He left his friend to dwell.
Let Virginia sing of Jackson and Lee
Let all the other States in praise of their generals
Join the strain,
But what more have they done than him
Who has lost his life for his country's gain?[54]

Chapter 5

War's Reality

1864

The New Year rang in with more screams for peace. A public meeting with over one thousand citizens was held on January 30, 1864, at the courthouse in Greensboro. It was felt "that the people have a right to assemble together to consult for their common good, to instruct their Representatives, and to apply to the Legislature for a redress of grievances."[55]

The large meeting was organized by James A. Long, chairman; Colonel Abram Clapp, vice-president; and William M. Mebane, secretary. On motion, Robert P. Dick, William S. Gilmer, Jesse Benbow, Jeremiah Clapp and John Gant were appointed to prepare business.

Robert P. Dick stated, "We as freemen of Guilford County

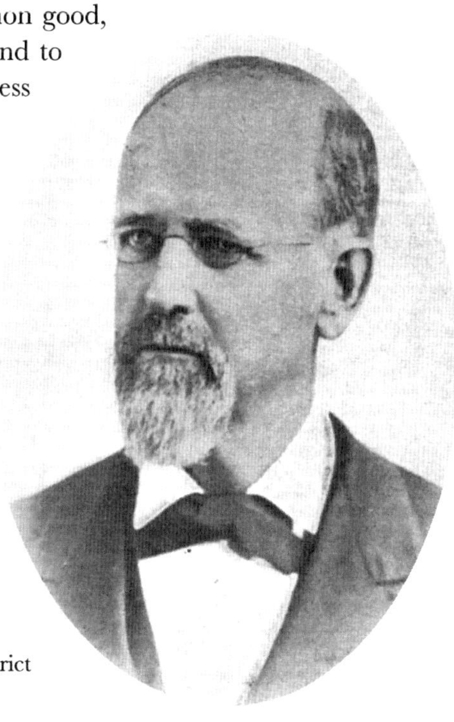

Robert Paine Dick, peace activist during the war, later served in the North Carolina Supreme Court and as a United States district judge. *Bettie Caldwell.*

and loyal citizens of North Carolina in public meeting assembled have the following opinions. 'That the people have a right to assemble.'"[56]

The *Greensborough Patriot* reported, "At the courthouse as soon as Robert P. Dick arose and amid such confusion from those in the gallery, he could not be heard. Appeals were made that peace and quiet be preserved and that was greeted by more hisses, whistling and disorder. Then Mr. D.F. Caldwell attempted to address and more noise rang out from the gallery."[57]

Robert P. Dick desired a state convention for peace though he professed honorable peace was impossible from Lincoln. He desired North Carolina in a convention with sister states of the South devise a way to stop the war as opposed to any separate state action. If other states refused to hear North Carolina's call for peace, then all might be assured they had done their duty to God and her people. Dick felt a strong peace party in the South would increase the power of peace men in the North and enable them to overturn the dynasty at Washington. If the conservative men of the North were in power, it was felt peace terms could be decided honorably for the entire country.

Dick said in a letter to the editor of the *Greensborough Patriot*, "I feel that it is a higher evidence of patriotism, to save the life of one citizen than to destroy a thousand enemies." Dick felt that if he had not been disturbed in his speech at the public meeting he could have given his views fully on all questions of public interest and felt he would have said nothing detrimental to the interest of the Confederate states.[58]

G. William Welker voiced his views at the meeting, which was reported in a newspaper article, "I am described as a Pennsylvania preacher. I have no reason to be ashamed of the land of my birth. Nearly all citizens of Guilford are descendants of those who emigrated from Pennsylvania—Scotch, Irish and German…I loved the old Union, I am for peace now."[59]

The people of Guilford County in the 1860s were great orators and writers, and the *Greensborough Patriot* printed long-winded debates between the people. Many people wrote in private under titles such as "A True Friend of North Carolina" or "One of the People."

The peace meeting became a mob, and the meeting ended.

> *But the boys and soldiers thought differently, and although the disturbances is to be regretted yet perhaps there is more excuse for the soldiers than we are ready to admit. They thought no doubt of Adams, Cole, Charles, Gorrell, Weatherly, and Weir—the young and the brave, who had gone down to bloody graves, in defense of the holy "soil of Guilford." They thought*

> *of the gallant* [John Alexander] *Gilmer, languishing in hearing of the meeting, from a wound almost mortal, received on the bloody field of Bristow. They thought of Guilford's numerous dead, buried in the land of the stranger—of her numerous sons now standing as living bulwarks between the "holy soil" of Guilford and its fiendish foes—they thought of their own exposure to cold, to hunger, to disease and death in the same holy cause and is it unnatural that their blood should boil with indignation at a proceeding which is calculated to encourage and strengthens our enemies, protract the war, and bring it upon the holy soil of Guilford.*
>
> *Submitted by: A True Friend of North Carolina.*[60]

Will L. Scott wrote, "A conscience void of offense should be man's highest ambition."[61] He felt it impossible to seek peace through Lincoln's administration. He desired that an effort be made to negotiate peace. He believed the route was to believe in God and pray, and he stated, "The Confederate Constitution declares, 'the right of the people peaceably to petition the government for a redress of grievances.'"[62]

Will's full name was William Lafayette Scott, a former colonel of the Twenty-first North Carolina and an attorney by profession. According to Scott, "Good government results from private and public virtue and all virtue is the offspring of gospel influences. This is a golden thought, which ought to be uppermost in every public man's mind."[63]

In a Raleigh newspaper, James A. Long was quoted as saying:

> *It is however to be much regretted that some who could have prevented all disorder and preserved peace and quiet, did not do so. I have simply to add in conclusion that the meeting on last Saturday has satisfied every intelligent man that so far as the people of Guilford are concerned, that while they are willing and ready to put forth all their energies in common with their fellow-citizens of the Confederacy to gain their independence, and to make a final separation from the North, yet they are not prepared, and will never submit to a military despotism at home, and will contend for the writ of habeas corpus under any and all circumstances.*[64]

In early January 1864, food for General Lee's army was lacking, while great amounts of provisions were at Greensboro and Charlotte awaiting enough railroad cars to handle the flow. Each day, ninety-four thousand rations were needed by Lee's army in Richmond and Petersburg.

Walter A. Thompson, state agent, was in Greensboro in early 1864 to gather boxes from home to deliver to the troops of the Army of Northern Virginia. Edward Warren, surgeon general of North Carolina, was in need of ten thousand pairs of gloves and socks for the troops.[65] In addition to agents, family and friends routinely sent care packages to their loved ones via soldiers returning to camp from furlough visits at home. Soldiers returning from furlough often carried letters back to the soldiers on the war front. Letter writing was a necessity and a comfort to the soldier far from home as well as the family anxiously waiting on the homefront. Great anxiety was suffered if the mail was delayed, and paper shortages were common.

In addition to sending care packages and letters to the soldiers in an effort to alleviate their suffering from lack of the basic necessities of life and news from home, efforts were made to create a pleasant resting place in Guilford County for the soldiers passing through the community. "A new soldiers' home in the form of a way-side [*sic*] hospital is established by Dr. Neagle. It is hoped the establishment will provide relief to weary soldiers on their journeys."[66]

The Ladies' Soldiers' Aid Society worked to assist the hospital personnel whenever their services were needed as evidenced by a public response from Dr. Neagle, published in the local paper:

> *Dr. J.L. Neagle, Assistance Surgeon in charge of the hospital, extends appreciation to the Ladies Soldiers' Aid Society for one shirt, one pair drawers and one pair of socks. He also received a bouquet of flowers and a wreath of evergreens from a lady friend to dress the body of Lieutenant W.W. Lane, Company A, 56th North Carolina who was killed in Greensboro after falling between the platform of the water tank and rail cars while they were in motion. He is the third soldier to meet* [an] *untimely death in such a manner. It is felt the chief train engineer should look into the safety of the rail platform.*[67]

The Barbee Hotel in High Point was converted to a wayside hospital and opened on September 1, 1863. The ladies of the High Point community offered their assistance to ease the burdens of the soldiers. One young lady, Laura Wesson, cared for soldiers afflicted with smallpox. The diseased soldiers were removed to a building some distance from High Point, and Wesson cared for them until she contracted the disease.[68]

Guilford County at this time in history was a bustle of activity and raging emotions. The Home Guard of Guilford County, Fourth Regiment, routinely gathered in Greensboro. Captains Holton, Armfield, Thom, Greason, Gardner, Pritchett, Wall, Kirkman, Rankin and Forbis commanded.[69]

A commission was established in Greensboro to help the suffering families in Guilford County as they fought hunger, and the commissioners, led by Jed H. Lindsay, attempted to alleviate the suffering. Food supplies continued to be difficult for the soldiers' families to obtain due to escalating costs, though warehouses in the community were overflowing with supplies intended for the soldiers. Foreign supplies, stored in warehouses in Greensboro, were a result of blockade runners successfully avoiding the enemy ships patrolling coastal North Carolina.

> *Major Sloan of this place, the present state quartermaster, within the last few days have been receiving large amounts of state supplies from abroad for NC troops. We learn Maj. Sloan has already several millions dollars' worth of stores on hand at this point. This is another piece of evidence at the foresight and the practical good sense of Gov. Vance in providing the wants and supplying the necessities of his gallant soldiers on the field.*[70]

The United States enjoyed a powerful navy, and the Confederacy realized supremacy on the waterways was key to military success. This supremacy ultimately contributed to the defeat of the Confederacy. Supplies were critically needed to aid the Southern war effort, and the Confederate treasury lacked funds to maintain enough ships on the waterways to defend the South. An attempt was made to create a private navy financed by patriotic entrepreneurs. The purpose was to weaken the United States Navy and seize its warships and commercial vessels laden with cargo intended for foreign trade for the benefit of the South. Each state of the Confederacy was expected to create a volunteer navy. The president of the North Carolina Volunteer Navy Company was a native of Guilford County. The concept of public ownership of a navy versus government ownership was an ingenious endeavor but came too late in the war to be much help: "North Carolina Volunteer Navy Company was organized January 14, 1864 with Cyrus P. Mendenhall, Esquire as president. Supposedly one million dollars was subscribed and a good portion of that was invested in Naval stores for exportation. Invitations are offered as shares are only 500 dollars each."[71]

Governor Vance received a request for slave labor from Honorable James A. Seddon, secretary of war of the Confederate States. Vance responded with the following explanation:

> *State of North Carolina, Executive Department, Raleigh, N.C., February 12, 1863.*

Hon. James A. Seddon, Secretary of War:

Sir: I have the honor to acknowledge the reception of your letter of the 4th instant, invoking the aid of the authorities of the State to procure labor for the completion of the Danville railroad, and also asking my influence with the Legislature in securing the gauge of that road to correspond with that of the Virginia road. The object is a most important one and commends itself strongly to my favor; but under all the circumstances I feel compelled to decline impressing slaves to aid in its completion. For many months past the eastern part of this State has been furnishing labor upon all the public works from Wilmington to Petersburg, and no less than twenty counties are now employing their slaves. In the region through which this road runs there are very few slaves, and the very existence of the people require them to labor on their farms. In addition to the fact that this road is viewed with almost universal disfavor in the State as entirely ruinous to many east of it, and that the charter never could have been obtained but as a pressing war necessity, I feel it due to candor that I should add there exists a very general impression here that upon the completion of the Danville connection, as it is termed, the eastern lines of our roads would be abandoned to the enemy. How far this opinion does injustice to the purpose of the War Department I am not able to say; I merely state the fact. For these reasons, with the additional one that this road is constructed by private contractors, I do not feel that I could be justified in forcing the labor of citizens upon it. I assure you I regret this exceedingly, not only on account of the importance of the work itself to our military operations, but also because it is exceedingly unpleasant for me to refuse to do anything whatsoever which is requested by the Confederate authorities and regarded as important to the general cause. I would suggest however, that a large number of free negroes might be obtained from the adjoining counties of Virginia and North Carolina, and if the species of labor could be made available, my assistance in gathering it up shall be promptly rendered. In regard to the gauge of the road, I have to say that the proposition to make it conform with the Virginia road had been disposed of in the negative before yours was received.

Very respectfully, your obedient servant, Z.B. Vance[72]

Ads in the paper at this time advertised for kitchen grease, lard, tallow, spoiled bacon, old copper and brass, cast steel, bacon, pork, corn and corn meal. "Highest cash prices will be paid at the Manassas Gap Rail Road Shops, near the depot, Greensborough, NC."[73]

The railroad cars ran daily from Danville, Virginia, to Reidsville, North Carolina. Captain J.L. Hawkins was the conductor. Unfinished grading was about six miles, and about eighteen miles of rail needed to be laid. Captain Morrow, the telegraph superintendent, reported removing old line and installing new line along the railroad. From Greensboro to the point of the railroad completion, wagons loaded with supplies and passengers were in continuous movement along the path of the railway.[74]

The first train, via the Piedmont Railroad, from Danville arrived in Greensboro on May 21, 1864, a distance of forty-five miles. With the completion of the railroad, the number of prisoners, refugees, troops and tragedies greatly increased. A large group of Yankee prisoners arrived in Greensboro via the Piedmont Railroad en route to the South. The prisoners were being transported to Georgia, and while at the station, three of them attempted escape. They were ordered to halt by the guards and refused. One prisoner was killed; the other two escaped.

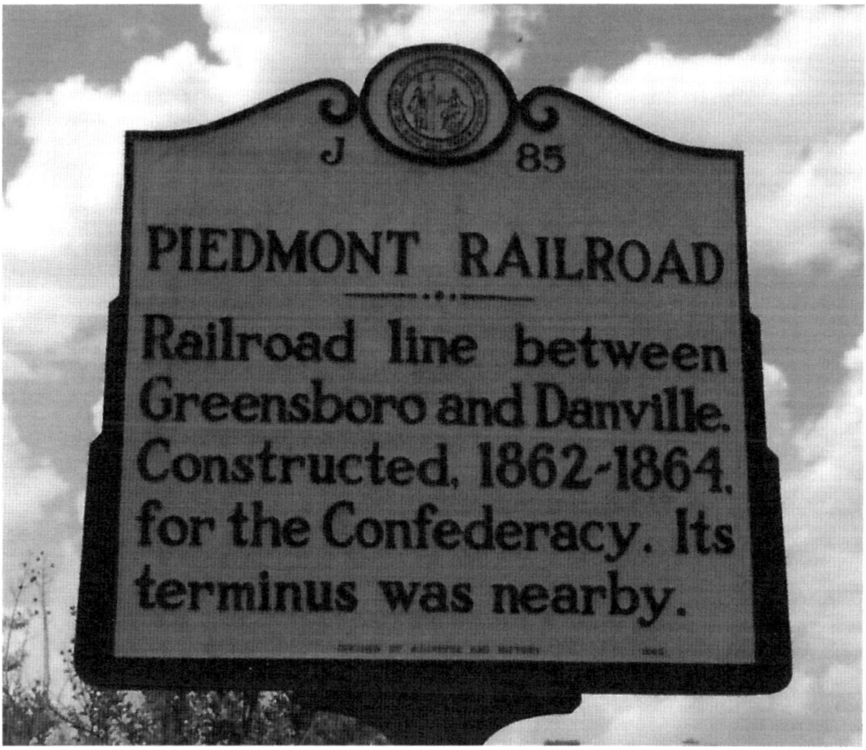

The Piedmont Railroad provided a needed route between Greensboro and Danville, Virginia, during the final months of the war. *Author's collection.*

Immediately after the completion of the railroad, complaints surfaced that troops were taking up the available space on the trains needed for transporting supplies.

Confederate postmaster general John H. Reagan created the Confederate postal system using similar methods in use by the United States Postal Service. Mail was so important to the South that upon completion of the Piedmont Railroad, specific times were established for transporting the mail. "Piedmont Rail Road Company: Mail and Accommodation trains leaving at 4:30 AM and 7 PM connect with the Southern train at Greensboro. The trains will depart Danville, Virginia at 4:30 AM for mail; accommodations at 7 pm and freight at 4:40 AM."[75]

A *Greensborough Patriot* editorial spoke of the illegal selling of alcohol as a nuisance, but an even greater nuisance was the passing of law to allow the sale of brandy to the public—at the same time the Piedmont Railroad completion made Greensboro a stop for a great number of soldiers.[76]

A soldier, Hinsdale, heading home to Waughtown was crushed at the railroad station. He attempted to jump onto the platform of a car while the train was in motion but, not gaining the platform, was carried to the woodshed. When between the woodshed and the car, he was crushed.

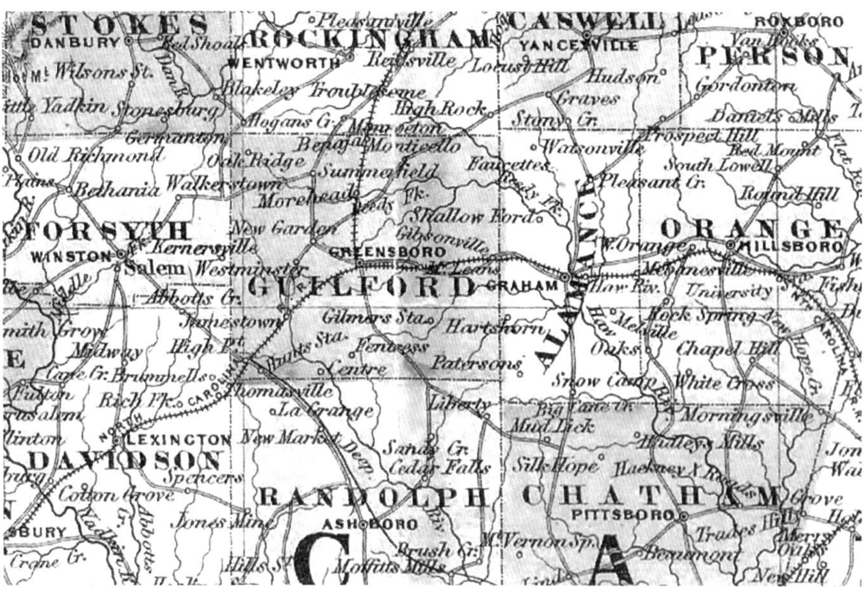

This map shows the route of the North Carolina Railroad and the Piedmont Railroad. *Courtesy of the State Archives of North Carolina.*

Fourth Battalion North Carolina Junior Reserves, Company A, was raised in Guilford County and mustered for service on May 22, 1864. In early 1865, this battalion was combined with other junior battalions to form the Third Regiment North Carolina Junior Reserves. Captain W.B. Johnson's Seventh Regiment Senior Reserves organized on June 18, 1864, in Guilford County consisting mostly of men from the county. Captain Jacob Boon's Company D organized on the same date and in the same place. James Robert McLean, a resident of Guilford County and a former member of the Confederate House of Representatives, served for a short period as major of the Seventh Regiment North Carolina Senior Reserves.[77] Most of these men were over the age of forty-five, and a few were over the age of fifty.

The battles in Virginia resulted in huge casualties. The Guilford Grays suffered the deaths of Samuel F. McLean and L.S. Lineberry. Wounded were Captain John A. Sloan, Sergeant W.U. Steiner, Sergeant Stratford, Corporal Klutt and Privates F.G. Chilcutt, D. Coltrain, W.H. Donnell, S.E.B. Gray, T.R. Greeson, W.A. Horney, S.S. Hiatt, William Hunt, James Hardin, R.B. McLean, L. May, William May, John Siler, R.B. Tate, W. Williams and James Wilson. A few of these men—all from the same company that originated in Guilford County—died from their wounds.

Lieutenant Samuel Hunter, Fifth Cavalry, died from wounds on June 12, 1864; his body arrived for interment in the soil of Guilford.[78] Though not always possible, attempts were made to bring the deceased home for burial. The soldiers of the Confederacy were dying on the battlefields and entire regiments were being decimated, increasing the need for replacements from younger and older white men, along with free persons of color.

The requirements for new recruits were published in the local paper:

> *Chief Enrolling Office, 6th, Cong Dist. Greensboro, April 8, 1864. In accordance with Circular No. 10 Conscript Office, Raleigh, N.C. of date March 28, 1864, county enrolling officers will enroll all white males between the ages of 17 and fifty years within the limits of their respective commands…Under Circular No. 9, Bureau of Conscription, March 19th, 1864. Enrolling officers are required to enroll all male free persons of color between the ages of 18 and 60 years. These free persons of color will be brought before the Medical Examination Board.*[79]

Guilford County was in turmoil. Arriving were the sick and wounded, the dead bodies of Guilford County's sons, United States prisoners of war, new recruits and refugees, but somehow life continued.

The continued demand for men from the community due to relentless military conscription stressed an already stressful situation for the women of Guilford County as they attempted to manage more farm work without the benefit of the physical strength the male population provided. The women persevered and tried to meet the demands the chaos of war inflicted upon them and, additionally, managed to meet the serious needs of the sick and wounded upon arrival in the community, as evidenced by this newspaper report highlighting the work of women:

> *Soldiers' relief societies are in operation in Greensboro. In 1864, the ladies focused on the wants of sick and wounded soldiers arriving in town. The Piedmont Railroad completion greatly increased the number. Rarely a train arrives from Danville that is not loaded with disabled and suffering soldiers. They arrive hungry and in need of attention, very pitiable. Ladies of the Soldiers' Aid Society organized a system of relief and attendance so they can attend to any number of people. The ladies are referred to as "sisters of mercy" waiting for the trains to arrive to perform their "humane and patriotic" duties. The ladies arrive with baskets full of food and offerings of smiles and sympathy. The number of soldiers tended in such a fashion at times to number in the 100's. Sick and wounded are passing through and hundreds are constantly in Greensboro at the three hospitals.*[80]

According to Mary Watson Smith, wife of a Presbyterian minister, when the Danville train arrived, it was "a signal to broil bacon, bake cornbread and set out all the milk one could lay hands on, the only delicacies we could then afford."[81]

Another Guilford Gray, Samuel F. McLean, died on May 5, 1864, during the Wilderness battle. His head received a piercing wound, killing him immediately. He was buried by his own brother beneath two huge oak trees by the roadside about a mile from the field on which he died. The newspaper memorialized him with the following poem:

> *Hushed within a lonely grave,*
> *Samuel sleeps in a strange land*
> *He died our struggling South to save,*
> *From a tyrant's bloody hand.*
> *He has crossed death's water o'er*
> *In answer to the angel's call*
> *The homestead threshold never more*
> *Will echo his footfall.*[82]

John W. Pitts's Company A, Fourth Battalion North Carolina Junior Reserves, organized on May 22, 1864, consisting mainly of seventeen-year-old farmers from Guilford County. Companies such as this one prepared young men to join other companies upon reaching the age of eighteen. Several men of this company were hospitalized in Wilmington, North Carolina, during the late summer and autumn of 1864 with bilious fever characterized by vomiting and diarrhea. Members of this company saw action along the eastern coast of North Carolina.

On May 5 and 6, 1864, soldiers from Guilford County participated in the Wilderness Campaign, and they fought at Graves' Farm on May 10 and at Spotsylvania Courthouse on May 12. Captain Sloan of the Guilford Grays stated, "We had now completed twelve days of battle at Spotsylvania, and at no time, day or night, did the firing on the lines entirely cease."[83]

At Pole Green Church on June 1, 1864, Lieutenant Charles A. Campbell was mortally wounded. His last words to Captain Sloan were, "Goodbye Captain; if I don't come back, tell them I fell fighting at the front."[84]

Lieutenant Samuel Hanner died in a Richmond, Virginia hospital from a gunshot wound to the abdomen he received in battle at Haw's Shop, Virginia. The newspaper reported: "Death of Lieut Hanner. The remains of Lieut Samuel Hanner of 5th Cavalry were brought home last Saturday night for interment, he having died of the wound received on the 12th. He was greatly respected by all who knew him."[85] Hanner was more fortunate than many of those from Guilford County who died on the bloody fields of battle because his remains were shipped home for burial. Many a soldier from Guilford County who died in battle remains buried in an unknown grave far from home.

The battles around Petersburg, Virginia, lasted from June 1864 until March 1865. The Confederate military moved captured Federal soldiers south; many of them passed through Guilford County, via the railroad. In June, "some 700 prisoners captured at Petersburg on Thursday last, reached here by the Piedmont road Saturday night. They say the entire army has lost all confidence in Grant, and desire McClellan to take command."[86]

The explosion at Petersburg, Virginia, and the devastating consequences shocked both the North and the South. Guilford County citizens were worried and concerned, especially due to the fact many of their loved ones were engaged in combat there.

The *Greensborough Patriot* reported:

> *At a late hour Saturday evening, we visited the chasm caused by the enemy's explosion. It appeared to be about 40 feet in depth, and some 200 feet in*

> *circumference, and resembled more where one would imagine to have been the effects of a terrible earthquake than anything else to which we could liken it. Immense boulders of earth were piled up rudely one above the other and great fragments of bomb…gun carriages, timbers, etc. were lying promiscuously in every direction. One man was caught between two boulders, near the surface of the grounds, and literally crushed between them. He still remained in this painful position, with only his head and neck visible, our men not having had the time to extricate him. Life had long been extinct but the ghastly looking face was unmarked by a scratch, and the head perfect, but lightly reclining on the shoulder. The sides and bottom of the chasm were literally lined with Yankee dead and the bodies lay in every conceivable point. In one spot we noticed a corporal of infantry, a sergeant of artillery and a big, burly Negro, piled one upon top of another. Some had evidently been killed with the butts of muskets, as their crushed skulls and badly mashed faces too plainly indicated, while the great portion were dead, great pools of blood having flowed from their wounds and stained the ground. Between our breastworks and the enemy's large numbers of dead and wounded were still lying, the latter begging piteously for water, and praying to be cared for. Our men could not relieve them as they were in full range of the enemy's sharpshooters, who had not ceased their firing, even under such appalling circumstances as we have described.*[87]

Captain John A. Sloan, Twenty-seventh North Carolina, Company B, engaged in battle at Petersburg and described the horrific scene:

> *Grant had constructed a mine under one of our forts in front of Petersburg, the main gallery of which was five hundred and twenty-two feet in length, with eight side galleries; in each of these galleries was placed about fourteen hundred pounds of powder. Gen. Burnside, in charge of this new feature of warfare, was to explode the "infernal machine," and walk into Petersburg with his colored troops, supposedly unmolested. About daylight on the morning of the 30th, this famous mine—afterwards known as the "crater"—was exploded with a great noise, as of a "rushing mighty wind, and there was a great earthquake, and the sun became black." About one hundred of our men and three or four guns were moved out of their places into the air, and when the smoke cleared away an opening about one hundred and fifty feet long, sixty feet wide, and thirty feet deep appeared in place of our earthworks. Simultaneously with this explosion the enemy opened a terrific fire along their whole front, and the white division selected for this occasion came slowly through the abattis up to this hole, where they were met by a merciless fire from our artillery, enfilading them right and left,*

> *with our infantry in their front. They were badly led, and, being demoralized, they faltered and sought shelter in the crater…and the "colored troops fought bravely," until the withering fire from our guns created a panic, when into the crater pell-mell they rushed, white and black, a disordered, mangled, quivering mass; our shot, shells, balls, and canister creating a perfect carnival of death. Some few endeavored to leave the crater and run back, but they were immediately shot down. Those who witnessed the scene say it was beyond the power of words to describe. Our lines were soon re-established, and our brigade was sent to relieve the troops holding the lines where the mine was sprung. Thus ended this "miserable affair."*
>
> *The space between the two lines, as now formed, was so close as to endanger any exposure whatever, and we had to hug our earthworks very closely. Our company was in line immediately at the crater. In our front, and almost under our noses, lay the bloated, festering bodies of their dead, exposed to the scorching rays of a July sun. To make our situation still more interesting, it was supposed that the battery on our right was also mined; and we were daily and nightly in fear of another explosion, and to be landed—no telling where. We remained in this position for a week, when Grant asked for a truce to bury his dead. We were then moved a short distance to our right, where we remained until about the middle of August. While on these lines, we literally lived under the ground. We had to pass to and from the front in covered ways; our rations were all prepared in the rear, and sent to us. We were compelled to sleep in bomb-proofs to avoid their mortar shells, with which they enlivened the scene at night.*[88]

Sergeant Daniel W. McConnell, already stricken and in a field hospital behind the line of battle, was paralyzed when a bomb struck near him. A family member arrived to care for him and returned home with his body after death. McConnell was buried in First Presbyterian Church Cemetery, location now unknown.

In September 1864, a group identifying itself as the Ladies' Hospital Association received food and money donations, including milk, butter, beans, potatoes, onions, flour, apples, corn, cakes, pies, molasses, cabbage, soup, bandages, buttermilk, peaches and money totaling $41.33. The ladies of Graham in adjoining Alamance County sent rice, vegetables and cash totaling $741.50.[89]

Donations continued: Mrs. Hildesheimer, beans; Mrs. Wayneck, chickens, peaches and sweet bread; Jane Ogburn, pickles, cucumbers, beans, potatoes and apples; James Paisley, beans and potatoes; Robert L. Stuart, flour,

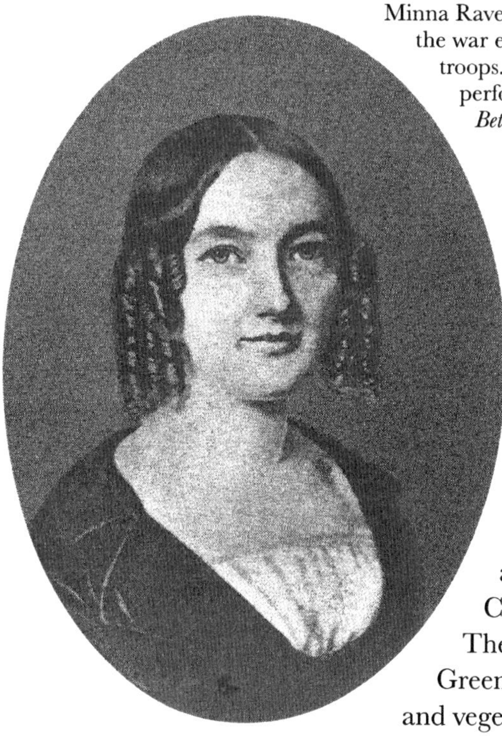
Minna Raven Hildesheimer assisted with the war effort by providing food for the troops. She also entertained with musical performances during the war years. *Bettie Caldwell.*

cabbage and cucumbers; A.M. Kerner, beans; Dr. J.A. McLean, beans; Jacob Clapp, potatoes; John C. Rankin, chicken; and J.R. Gilmer, beans and molasses. A special box was received from J.R. Bullock of Townsville, North Carolina, and Dr. W.S. Edwards of Chatham County sent butter. The Hospital Association of Greensboro received more fruit and vegetables.

In late September, *the Greensborough Patriot* published the following announcement: "Announced from headquarters, 6th Congressional District, an order for all men between the ages of 17 and 50. Additionally free Negroes age 18 to 50 are included in the call."[90]

General Sherman, United States, knew the great value of Greensboro, with its commissary and quartermaster's stores. The Piedmont Railroad was running at full capacity, but the supplies that General Lee needed for his army were accumulating. An informant by the name of Mr. Lamb, a resident of Guilford County, related to the enemy that at Greensboro there were only about one hundred guards. Lamb also informed the enemy there were no troops between Guilford County and the Tennessee state line, except for about fifty men in each county whose duties were to arrest deserters and enforce conscription. It was felt the stores at Greensboro were of immense value and could be destroyed easily by an assault from Petersburg, Virginia, or East Tennessee.[91]

In 1864, Camp Vance, near Morgantown, North Carolina, was closed, resulting in the opening of Camp Stokes near Greensboro on the road (now Battleground Avenue) leading to Martinsville, the first county seat of Guilford. The Sixty-seventh Militia was enrolling recruits. Camp Stokes was referred to as a place of assignment for conscripts, military training camp and a prison for deserters. Major Jesse R. McLean of Guilford County was in charge. The camp was named in honor of Colonel Montford Sidney Stokes, killed near Richmond.[92] Stokes was wounded at Ellerson's Mill, Virginia, on June 26, 1862, and died the following month. Before his service in the Confederacy, Colonel Stokes had a long military career. He served in a North Carolina regiment during the Mexican War and served in the United States Navy.[93]

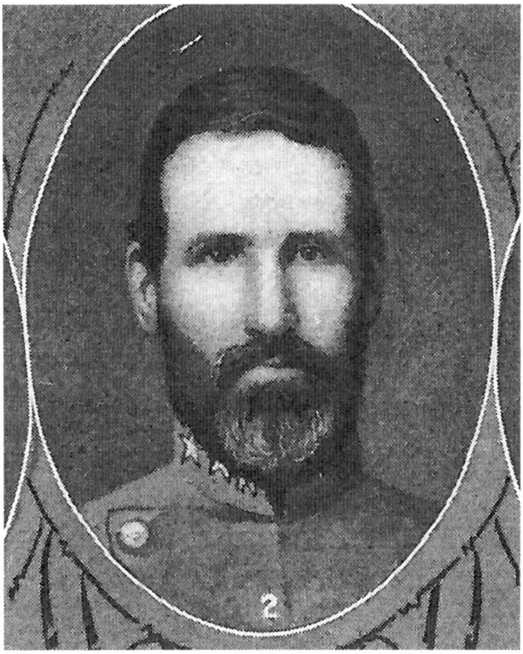

Camp Stokes, a camp of instruction in Guilford County, was named in honor of Colonel Montford Sidney Stokes, shown here. From Walter Clark's *Histories of the Several Regiments and Battalions from North Carolina in the Great War 1861–1865, Written by Members of Their Respective Commands.*

McLean's Battalion North Carolina Light Duty Men, under the command of Major Jesse R. McLean at Camp Vance, organized in 1864. A portion of Company A enlisted at Camp Vance at Morgantown, and once Camp Vance closed, the rest of the company enlisted at Camp Stokes in Guilford County in late 1864. Company B organized in January 1865 at Camp Stokes. These soldiers were in some way too disabled for active duty but able to serve as guards.

Harrison Church, described as a bushwhacker, along with two of his brothers, was captured by the Wilkes County Home Guard and sent to Camp Stokes.[94] A bushwhacker during the Civil War often stayed hidden in the woods near his home and engaged in guerrilla warfare, often for sustenance.

At Camp Stokes, James R. Bell died of pneumonia in the twenty-fifth year of his life. He was feeble in health and worked at hospitals in Richmond and Greensboro.[95] Typhoid fever, diarrhea, scurvy, smallpox, dysentery, measles and consumption were some of the diseases the soldiers suffered with, and in many cases, the diseases were as deadly as any weapons of war.

The young men of Guilford County were engaging in nonstop war in 1864. For example, the Guilford Grays, also known as the Twenty-seventh North Carolina, Company B, fought at Wilderness, Virginia, on May 5 and May 6, 1864; Graves' Farm, Virginia, on May 10; Attlee's Station, Virginia, on May 10; Spotsylvania Courthouse on May 12; Pole Green Church, Virginia, on June 2; Second Cold Harbor on June 3; Gary's Farm, Virginia, on June 15; Yellow Tavern, Virginia, on August 21; Ream's Station on August 25; and Bellfield, Virginia, on December 9.[96]

The Young Ladies' Knitting Society met twice a month in Greensboro. Its mission was to supply the soldiers with socks, and each lady was required to bring a sock, made by her own hands, to each meeting. Julia W. Stevenson, Lethe H. Lindsay, Cammie Rhodes and Mollie A. Gretter were officers of the organization.[97]

On December 15, 1864, over 150 cars of freight were in the government warehouse and twenty cars worth on the siding in Greensboro. In the previous week, an average of fifteen cars a day were leaving Greensboro for Danville. Agitation rose as some felt the Piedmont Road should have been taken under government control or the North Carolina Railroad should have handled the Piedmont Road, which would have alleviated the problem of trains from Charlotte having a delay at Greensboro; they could continue on to Danville. Supplies waiting delivery were accumulating in Greensboro.

Ladies of the Note Signing Bureau in Columbia, South Carolina, traveled on the trains and arrived in Greensboro in the middle of the night. Nevertheless, they were greeted by the ladies of the town and treated in a hospitable manner.

At the close of 1864, the government authorized the seizure of the railroad and all its assets. An order from the Confederate government concerning the Piedmont Railroad stated, "Major S.R. Chisman, Quartermaster, on the behalf of the Confederate States will seize and impress the road and turn it over to the Quartermaster-General."[98]

The impressment of the railroad came too late to have any effect. While food sat rotting in warehouses, Lee's army was starving—and so were many people in Guilford County.

Chapter 6

War Concludes

1865

Robert P. Dick continued to promote peace, as evidenced in the *Greensborough Patriot* in January 1865:

> *Permanent peace, prosperity and happiness of both the North and the South depend upon a close and friendly alliance. For more than three years we have strained every nerve and put forth every energy; we have fought more than three hundred battles, won much of the glory of victory at a fearful cost, and still have not gained our independence, or even foreign sympathy and recognition…Where now are our noble heroes who so often bore their battle flags to victory, and won so many trophies of triumph? Many of them lie buried in a foreign land, and the mounds of the battle-field and the unmarked hillocks beside the hospital were the last resting places of the brave and the mourning desolation of tens of thousands of homes tell us that the loved and gallant ones will never come back again. Most of our citizens between eighteen and forty-five years of age, have gone to the front…it now tears the seventeen year-old* [sic] *boy from his mother's arms and takes the man with a half-century of years upon him from the midst of his helpless and weeping grandchildren…The conscript law has been enforced with merciless severity and even women and children have not escaped the rigors of its execution.*[99]

Dick felt there must be complete emancipation of slaves and not just those who enlisted in the Confederate military:

> *After the war, would the freed slave turned soldier return back to his wife and children still in bondage? The cornfield is the only battleground where the Negro can assist us in winning our independence; and we need him there to protect us from famine, an enemy more powerful than the Yankee, and more insatiably cruel than the most barbarous savage. Thousands of wives and children, widows and orphans of our brave soldiers will be crying in vain for bread.*
>
> *My voice is for negotiation and peace. The question may well be asked, what kind of a peace do you desire? To this inquiry my answer is direct and unequivocal. I will be content with any peace which the free enlightened and patriotic people of the South will say in the majesty of their power and sovereignty, is honorable and for the best interests of the nation. They have sustained the country thus far with their labor, their property, and their blood, and I am willing to trust them in everything. The messages, letters and declarations of Mr. Davis and Mr. Lincoln satisfy me that they will never effect a negotiation for peace. Their pride of consistency and intense hatred will always prevent them from acting together as peace makers, and must the two nations continue to pour out rivers of blood and tears to minister to the pride, ambition and obstinacy of their rulers? Successful efforts at negotiation can only be made by the sovereign States, and they ought to act together, and act immediately… If the States have a right to adopt measures to make war and to prevent war, they certainly have the power to appoint commissioners to tender a conference for negotiating a peace.*[100]

In Greensboro, James Sloan, major and chief commissary of subsistence, complained in a letter to Colonel L.B. Northrop, commissary-general at Richmond, Virginia, that his officers had no money to secure supplies because the producers refused to sell, feeling the Confederate government would not pay them.[101]

In early 1865, hospital attendants were desperately trying to secure enough supplies to treat the soldiers. J. Rankin Wilkinson, hospital steward at Confederate States of America General Hospital Number 12, in Greensboro, wrote to the *Patriot*, "Will the ladies save and send to this Hospital some old cotton and linen rags to dress the wounds of our suffering soldiers?"[102] Meanwhile, H. Holmes Hunter, surgeon in charge at Confederate States Way Hospital Number 2, also in Greensboro, requested from the ladies "seeds so a large garden can be cultivated for the benefit of the sick and wounded soldiers at the hospital."[103]

The situation became especially acute after the Battle of Bentonville in March 1865, when hundreds upon hundreds of wounded soldiers were put on the trains bound for points all along the railroad. Greensboro and High Point received more wounded soldiers than the towns could handle, filling churches, schools, halls and private residences to capacity. When Richmond, Virginia, was threatened by Federal troops, the Confederate leadership, including President Jefferson Davis, arrived in Greensboro via the Piedmont Railroad. The trains from Richmond also carried sick and wounded soldiers. The ladies met the challenge and cared for the wounded and members of the Confederate government, gathering what food items they could muster and serving them along with whatever they could spare from their own dwindling supplies.

Mary Watson Smith recalled the arrival in Greensboro of the soldiers from the Battle at Bentonville:

> *But it was on March 19, 1865, that war in its stern and startling reality came to our very doors. On that memorable night, without warning or preparation, the wounded were brought to Greensboro in such numbers as to fill the court house* [sic]*, the churches, and every available space in town. To that call, the women of Greensboro responded nobly and with one accord. All else was forgotten as with eager hand and tender heart they sought to make the poor fellows comfortable in their hastily improvised beds and comfortless quarters. In this mighty emergency, the town was at once divided into districts, and the women from each neighborhood fed from their own tables the numbers of men nearest them. In the old Presbyterian Church and lecture room, I saw the first wounded and dying men and witnessed the grief of their comrades. When I went back next morning, death had set its seal on many a noble form as they lay in a semicircle around the pulpit in the last long sleep that knows no waking nor rude alarms of war. But more pitiful than all was the absence of anesthesia. Yet, in this painful lack of equipment, the ingenuity and self-sacrifice, the sympathy and resourcefulness of our women made what amends were possible. Daily their interest in these dear men grew, as out of their own poverty they ministered to their need. But supplies of every kind in the South were alarmingly low, and none were coming in; and, all unawares to these devoted workers, the Confederacy of their love was tottering to its fall.*[104]

Smith's son, O. Norris Smith, recalled planks laid across the pews to hold the soldiers. Each soldier was laid on a blanket and covered with another blanket. Smith's son also related that he went with his mother each morning to carry water, towels and food. Each day, the dead soldiers were covered with blankets and placed in front of the pulpit. He recalled seeing dead soldiers placed in back of the church cemetery but could not say with certainty that they were buried there, though he thought they were buried close together.[105]

Confederate wounded in Greensboro were placed at the First Presbyterian and Methodist churches, the courthouse, Odd Fellows Hall, Britton Hotel, Garrett's Building and available homes. Arthur P. Ford relates in his book, *Life in the Confederate Army and Some Experiences and Sketches*:

> *At Greensboro, the courthouse was used as the hospital, all the benches, desks, etc., being removed. We had no mattresses, nor bedding of any kind, and about 200 of us were laid off in rows on the floor, with only our blankets that we brought with us. After looking over the accommodations, I selected the platform inside of the rail, where the judge's desk used to be, for my place, and went out into the street and begged an armful of hay from a wagon, and with two brick for a pillow made my bed. Here I lay for about three weeks with fever and at times very ill. Three times a day the ladies of the town came and brought us food, and were devoted in their attentions.*

In early April, the need for donations for the sick and wounded soldiers escalated, and the county folks responded by sending seven chickens; two turkeys; two gallons of milk; eight dozen eggs; 40 pounds of ham; 16 pounds of beef; 145 pounds of bread, cakes and pies; 3 pounds of butter; a peck of potatoes; one-half bushel of apples; a jar of peaches; a bushel of turnips; 3 pounds of soup; 2 pounds of soap; and two bottles of wine.[106]

On April 3, 1865, General Beauregard wrote to General Robert E. Lee at Petersburg, Virginia, and General Joseph E. Johnston at Smithfield, North Carolina, that he did not have enough guards to protect Greensboro, Salisbury and Danville. Cavalry was lacking, and the slowness of transportation limited him sending troops to reinforce Danville, Virginia. General Beauregard informed President Davis that he would send 600 men to Danville and had 2,500 more he had retained at Greensboro, if needed.[107]

There was much concern regarding the whereabouts of Federal general George Stoneman, and residents feared he might target Greensboro, which was his plan if the war continued long enough. General Beauregard was retaining troops, requesting artillery to move to Greensboro and inquiring if cavalry was available to seek out Stoneman's troops.[108]

On April 9, 1865, General Lee surrendered the Army of Northern Virginia at Appomattox Court House. While at Danville, President Davis, having fled Richmond on April 2, notified General Johnston that General Lee had surrendered. Johnston notified Secretary of War John C. Breckinridge in Danville that General Sherman was marching to Raleigh. General Beauregard expected an attack on the Danville Railroad and most likely Greensboro.

Athos, a pen name for an anonymous writer, recorded the horror of the surrender of General Lee's Army of Virginia in a newspaper article published after the war:

> *The hearts of the Southern people were wrung with grief, their heads were bowed with sorrow. Vain were all their struggles, vain were all their losses; vain were all their suffering; vain were all their dead. Did you ever see a nation weep? Did you ever hear the wail of a great people? Did you ever hear of a general calamity? Did you ever see sorrow and woe? I have, I saw the Confederacy weep when Robt. E. Lee folded the "Bonnie Blue Flag" and shed tears in the midst of his men. I heard the wail of the South when her proud Capital was wrapped in the embrace of consuming fire, and her streets echoed the tramp of foes. I have seen sorrow and woe sitting in the heart and soul of the Southern Goddess of Liberty.*[109]

The Confederate treasury and the Virginia State treasury were loaded onto rail cars via the Piedmont Railroad, while the North Carolina state treasury traveled on the North Carolina Railroad headed toward Guilford County. Rumors persist to this day that some of the Confederate gold and silver, valued in the millions, was buried in various places along the railroad tracks. Documentation exists that nearly $100,000 of gold was taken by soldiers of an Ohio cavalry.[110]

On April 10, Major J.C. Holmes was instructed by General Beauregard to hold all troops for defense of Greensboro and High Point. The military authorities attempted to defend Greensboro from possible attacks from Federal Major General George Stoneman and General Sherman's troops. The Confederate authorities expected attacks from either or both of the invaders.

Major General George Stoneman invaded North Carolina with his cavalry. The railroads supplying the Confederacy were one of his objectives. Stoneman turned his attention toward Greensboro and struck the North Carolina Railroad. He sent about one hundred men to destroy the Piedmont Railroad Bridge over Reedy Fork in Guilford County, moments after

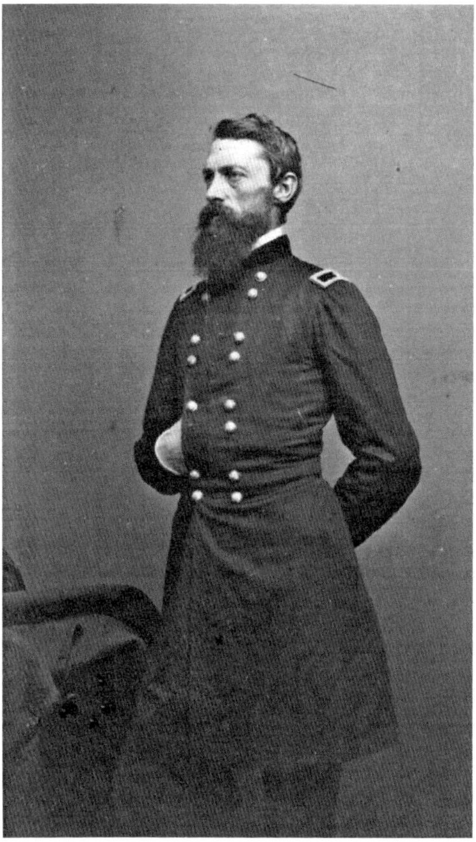

Major General George Stoneman, shown, and General Sherman were equally feared by the residents of Guilford County. *Library of Congress.*

Jefferson Davis and his cabinet had passed.[111]

On April 10, 1865, Stoneman ordered Colonel William J. Palmer to take control of Salem in neighboring Forsyth County and destroy the railroads. To accomplish these duties the following day, Colonel Palmer divided his men into four groups. A detachment under Lieutenant Colonel Charles Betts defeated a South Carolina cavalry guarding the North Carolina Railroad just a couple miles from Greensboro. Betts successfully burned the North Carolina Railroad bridge over South Buffalo Creek. After the war, Betts received a Medal of Honor for his service in Guilford County. He captured an entire battalion of Confederate troops on April 19, 1865. Meanwhile, Palmer sent Captain Adam Kramer to Jamestown. The Confederate stores there were destroyed, along with a warehouse and the North Carolina Railroad Bridge over Deep River. Two rail cars of medical and commissary supplies were confiscated, the train depot at High Point was destroyed and 1,700 bales of cotton, the property of Francis Fries of Salem, was destroyed.

On the evening of April 11, General Johnston ordered General Beauregard to send one hundred railroad cars to Raleigh to remove stores to Greensboro. Six hundred additional troops were sent to Greensboro to protect the town.[112]

President Davis, along with his cabinet, arrived in Greensboro on April 11 via the Piedmont Railroad. Davis's wife, Varina, and his children had passed through Guilford County on their way south prior to Davis's arrival. There are varying accounts of where Davis stayed while in Greensboro, and there is probably some truth in each account. It is known Davis stayed in a railroad car but was invited to stay at nearby homes. John Taylor Wood, a nephew of Davis through his first marriage to Sarah Knox Taylor, rented a home and moved his refugee family to Greensboro. It is a certainty the home was offered to Davis, given the close personal and political relationship between Wood and Davis. Supposedly, the landlord became very upset over the situation, fearing General Sherman's troops might destroy his property. Wood's story is similar to that of many others who enlisted in the Confederate military. He served in the United States Navy after graduating from the Naval Academy. Upon his return, he served as an instructor there. Wood served in the Confederate navy, notably as an officer onboard the *Virginia* when it engaged the *Monitor* in battle in 1862. Wood served as an aide to Jefferson Davis toward the close of war.[113]

A home known as Scarborough was rumored to shelter President Davis at some point during his stay. John M. Morehead supposedly offered his home, Blandwood, and George A. Trenholm, too sick to stay in the rail car, stayed there. Charles G. Memminger and his wife also took shelter there.

Davis related that he stayed at "my quarters in a house occupied by Col. J. Taylor Wood's family" located on Elm Street.[114] Amid fears of retaliation, Davis more than likely made brief appearances at many of the homes in Greensboro but chose the railroad car to protect the residences from possible destruction by the Yankees.

Former Secretary of War Mallory provided a bit of clarification on Davis's lodgings when he mentioned a cabinet meeting held in Greensboro:

> *At 8 o'clock that evening* [April 13, 1865] *the cabinet, with the exception of Mr. Trenholm whose illness prevented his attendance, joined the President at his room. It was a small apartment, some twelve by sixteen feet, containing a bed, a few chairs, and a table, with writing materials, on the second floor of the small dwelling of Mrs. John Taylor Wood; and a few minutes after eight the two generals entered. The uniform habit of President Davis, in cabinet meetings, was to consume some little time in general conversation before entering upon the business of the occasion, not unfrequently* [sic] *introducing some anecdote or interesting episode, generally some reminiscence of the early life of himself or others in the army, the Mexican war, or his Washington experiences; and his manner of relating and his application of them were at all times very happy and pleasing.*

Few men seized more readily upon the sprightly aspects of any transaction, or turned them to better account; and his powers of mimicry, whenever he condescended to exercise them, were irresistible. Upon this occasion, at a time when the cause of the Confederacy was hopeless, when its soldiers were throwing away their arms and flying to their homes, when its Government, stripped of nearly all power, could not hope to exist beyond a few days more, and when the enemy, more powerful and exultant than ever, was advancing upon all sides, true to his habit, he introduced several subjects of conversation, not connected with the condition of the country, and discussed them as if at some pleasant ordinary meeting. After a brief time thus spent, turning to General Johnston, he said, in his usual quiet, grave way, when entering upon matters of business: "I have requested you and General Beauregard to join us this evening, that we might have the benefit of your views upon the situation of the country. Of course, we all feel the magnitude of the moment. Our late disasters are terrible, but I do not think we should regard them as fatal. I think we can whip the enemy yet, if our people will turn out. We must look at matters calmly, however, and see what is left for us to do. Whatever can be done must be done at once. We have not a day to lose." A pause ensued, General Johnston not seeming to deem himself expected to speak, when the President said: "We should like to hear your views, General Johnston." Upon this the General, without preface or introduction—his words translating the expression which his face had worn since he entered the room—said, in his terse, concise, demonstrative way, as if seeking to condense thoughts that were crowding for utterance: "My views are, sir, that our people are tired of the war, feel themselves whipped, and will not fight. Our country is overrun, its military resources greatly diminished, while the enemy's military power and resources were never greater, and may be increased to any desired extent. We cannot place another large army in the field; and, cut off as we are from foreign intercourse, I do not see how we could maintain it in fighting condition if we had it. My men are daily deserting in large numbers, and are taking my artillery teams to aid their escape to their homes. Since Lee's defeat they regard the war as at an end. If I march out of North Carolina, her people will all leave my ranks. It will be the same as I proceed south through South Carolina and Georgia, and I shall expect to retain no man beyond the by-road or cow-path that leads to his house. My small force is melting away like snow before the sun, and I am hopeless of recruiting it. We may, perhaps, obtain terms which we ought to accept."

The tone and manner, almost spiteful, in which the General jerked out these brief, decisive sentences, pausing at every paragraph, left no doubt as to

> *his own convictions. When he ceased speaking, whatever was thought of his statements—and their importance was fully understood—they elicited neither comment nor inquiry. The President, who, during their delivery, had sat with his eyes fixed upon a scrap of paper which he was folding and refolding abstractedly, and who had listened without a change of position or expression, broke the silence by saying, in a low, even tone: "What do you say, General Beauregard?" "I concur in all General Johnston has said," he replied.*[115]

On April 11, President Davis in Greensboro communicated with Governor Vance in Raleigh that he had not heard from General Lee and had little hope from his army. Davis desired to meet with Vance and was optimistic that if the army held its position, scattered soldiers would return and the army would gather strength.[116]

Mary Watson Smith remarked upon Davis's arrival, "I am just from the depot where I had the pleasure of seeing President Davis and hearing his little address, and had the distinguished honor of serving him a cup of coffee which he very graciously drank out of my silver cup. Long will this day be remembered!"[117]

General Johnston established his headquarters one and a quarter miles to the west of Greensboro.[118] Lieutenant General Alexander P. Stewart established his camp a few miles east of Greensboro.[119] Many of the troops camped near the tracks of the North Carolina Railroad, along what is known today as Burlington Road (Highway 70).

President Lincoln was fatally wounded at Ford's Theater in Washington on April 14; he died the following day. Vice

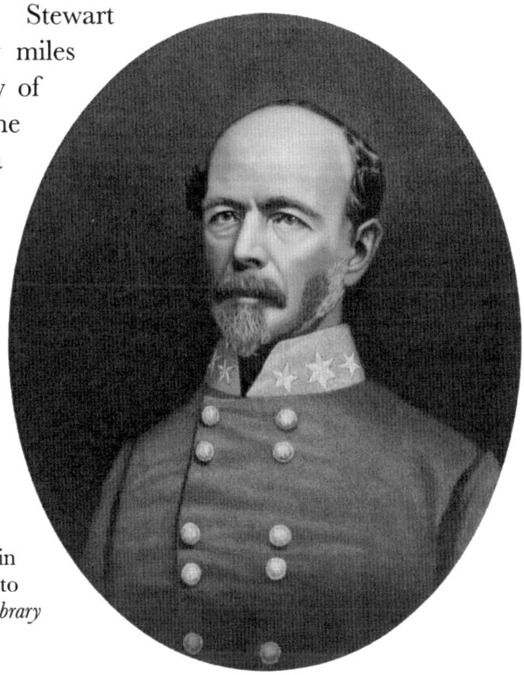

General Joseph E. Johnston served in the United States military previous to serving in the Confederate army. *Library of Congress.*

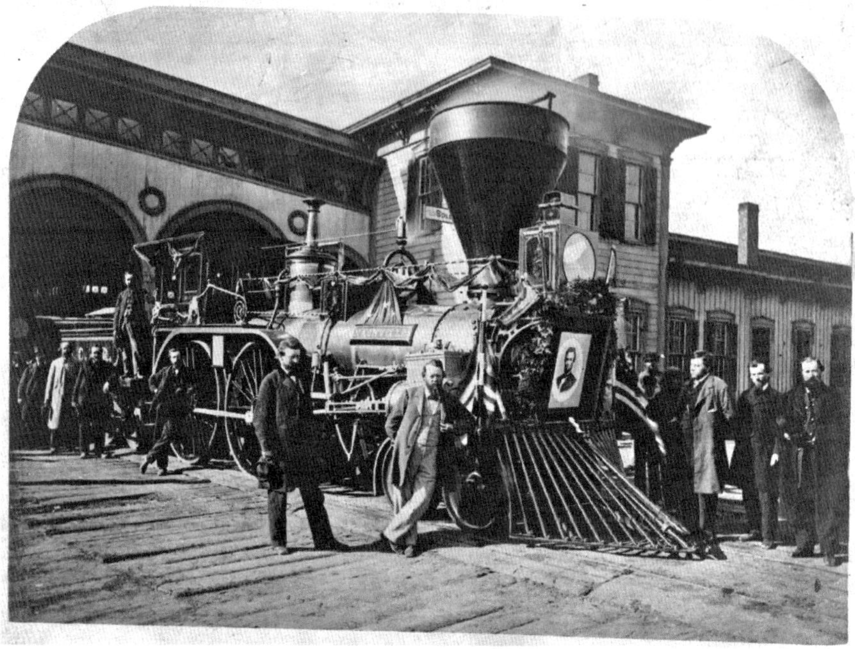

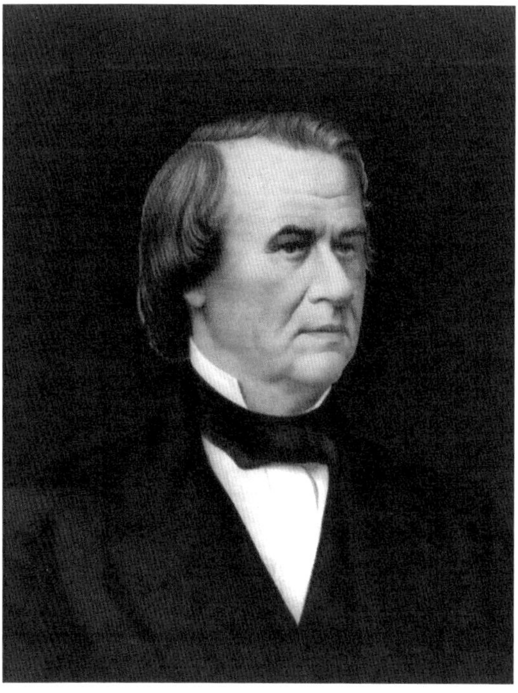

Above: Railroads played a key role for both the North and the South during the war. Shown is President Lincoln's funeral train. *Library of Congress.*

Left: Vice President Andrew Johnson became the seventeenth president of the United States upon the death of President Abraham Lincoln. *Library of Congress.*

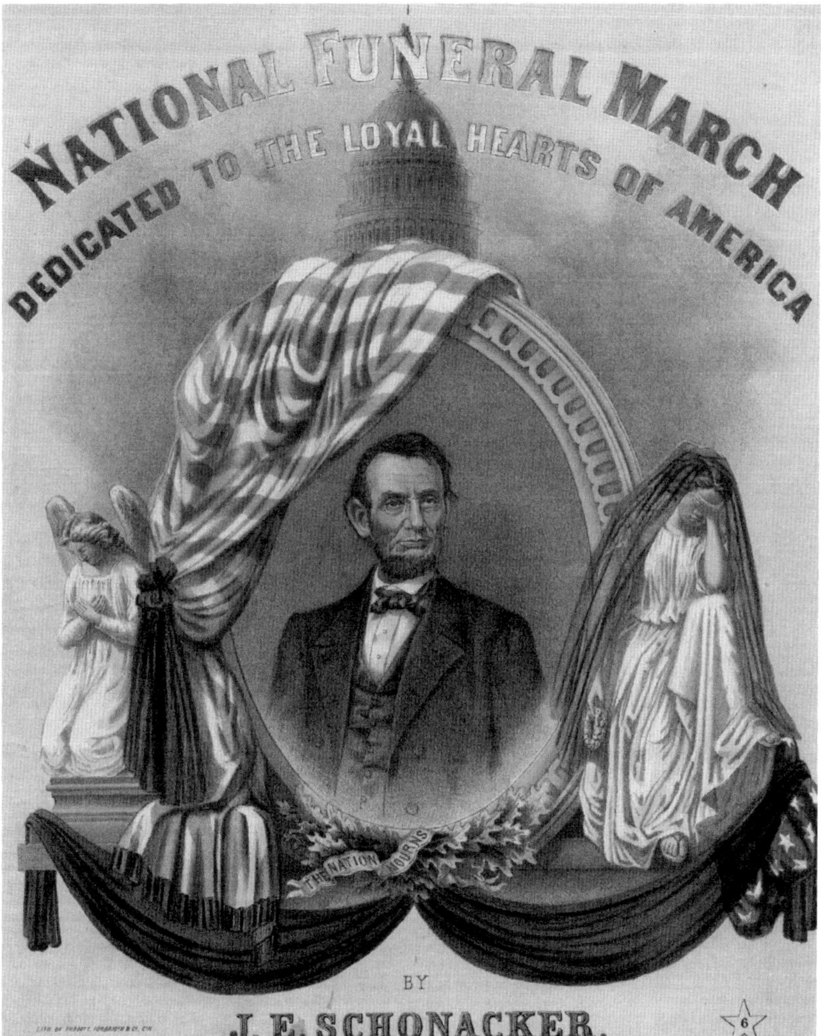

The assassination of President Abraham Lincoln shocked and saddened the people of both the North and the South. *Library of Congress.*

President Andrew Johnson was sworn in as the seventeenth president of the United States.

On April 15, President Davis left Greensboro, fleeing south. The governor of North Carolina, Zebulon Baird Vance, fled Raleigh ahead of General Sherman's advancing troops and arrived on April 16 in Greensboro, where he continued his duties as governor of the state.

Greensboro, at least temporarily, was the location of the state capital as well as the Confederate capital.

In a dispatch to General Johnston on April 18, 1865, General Beauregard requested that he negotiate the right to march the troops home and muster them out of service so the regimental colors could be deposited in the respective state capitols for preservation.[120] General Beauregard was well aware of the reverence the Confederate soldiers had for their regimental colors, having defended the flag during four years of war and watching countless comrades die in battle while protecting the colors.

On April 19, 1865, near Greensboro, Headquarters of Army of Tennessee, General Order No. 14 declared, "It is announced to the army that a suspension of arms has been agreed upon pending negotiations between the two governments. During its continuance the two armies are to occupy their present positions. By command of General Johnston, Archer Anderson, Lieutenant-Colonel and Assistant Adjutant-General."[121]

Governor Vance wrote General Johnston that his troops were forcibly seizing property belonging to North Carolina from Greensboro to the Haw River Depot in Alamance County. He informed General Johnston that General Sherman offered to safeguard the archives and funds of North Carolina if they were returned to Raleigh. Secretary of War Breckinridge seemed to take offense at Vance's request and retorted back in a letter to him that until an agreement was reached, it was better for Confederate troops to protect the property of the state of North Carolina rather than the enemy.[122]

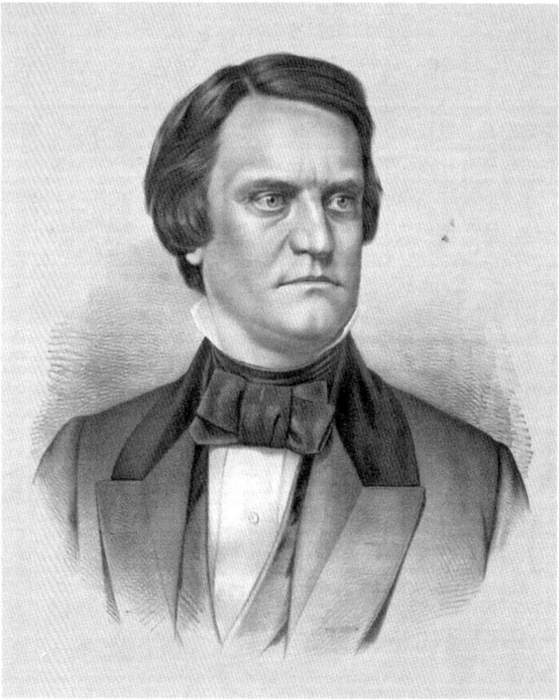

John Cabell Breckinridge, former vice president of the United States, served the Confederacy as secretary of war in 1865. *Library of Congress.*

Governor Vance seemed to be at odds with the Confederate government regarding North Carolina and the state's property, and he wrote to General Johnston, "Feeling, therefore, that I was to be excluded from a voice in the decision of the fate of my own people, I thought I could reasonably expect to be informed of the conclusion arrived at by others and make such provision as remained in my power for the welfare of the State…Very respectfully, your obedient servant, Z.B. Vance."[123]

In Greensboro, Major James Sloan, chief state quartermaster, reported over two hundred bales of blankets, cloth and ready-made clothing. The troops were issued over sixteen thousand yards of cloth, over four thousand pairs of pants, two thousand pairs of socks and over 1,100 jackets. Mobs violently seized the remainder of the Confederate stores. Many records of the quartermaster were destroyed.

All along the North Carolina Railroad, supplies were being ransacked. Governor Vance witnessed a train being sacked at McLean's Station (McLeansville) on April 19, 1865:

> *I myself saw the conclusion of the sacking of a train at McLean's Station yesterday morning by soldiers laden with blankets and leather. The cars had just been emptied as I got there, and the roadside and the woods were crowded with soldiers staggering under heavy loads of the plunder. It seemed to be an understood and permitted matter, as officers of nearly all grades were standing quietly around.*[124]

At McLean's Station, Major Melton, quartermaster of General Hampton's Corps, received stores and blankets from the railway cars, and having no source to haul the goods, his men carried the goods.[125] The commissary stores at McLean's Station were destroyed mainly to keep the supplies from falling into enemy hands. A rail car of shells exploded, and barrels of molasses and whiskey were leaking. "Hungry women dipped up molasses from the gutters in buckets. Hopeless men lapped up the liquor like dogs."[126] Governor Vance was very concerned about North Carolina's losses because, with the fall of the Confederacy, there would be no resource from which to seek restitution.

Due to correspondence between Union general Sherman and Confederate general Johnston, a cease-fire occurred to negotiate peace. On April 21, the president of the United States disapproved of the results. Another meeting took place on April 26, resulting in the surrender of General Johnston's Army of Tennessee. The terms were essentially the same as the terms offered General Lee at Appomattox.[127]

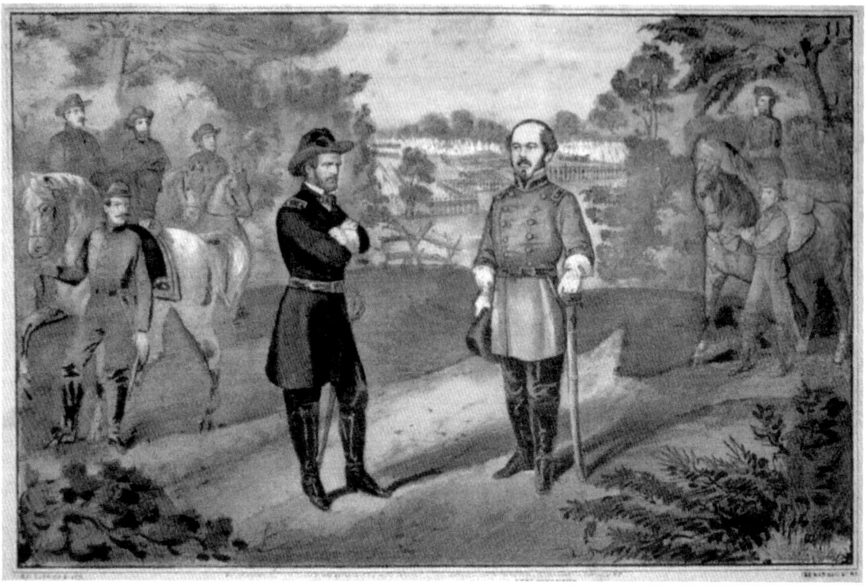

General Joseph E. Johnston surrendered his Army of Tennessee in North Carolina on April 26, 1865. *Library of Congress.*

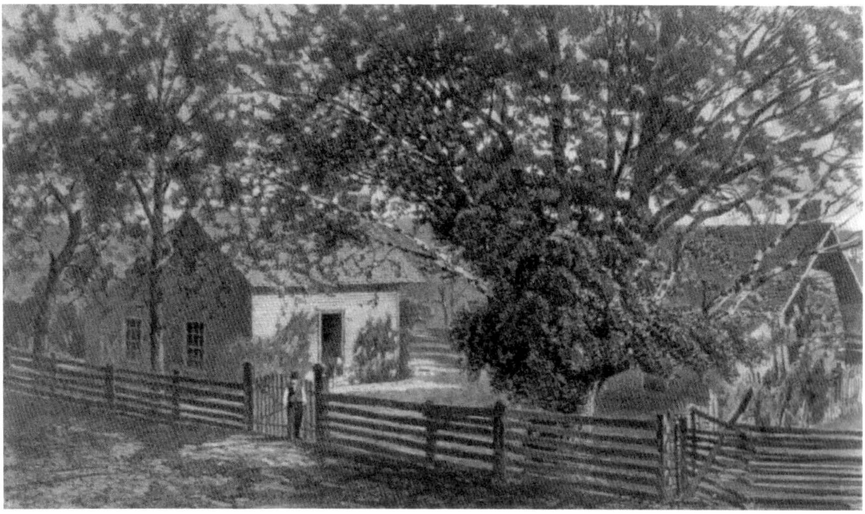

The Bennett house was the location for a meeting between General Joseph E. Johnston and Union general William Sherman to end hostilities. *Library of Congress.*

On April 27, 1865, it was ordered that guns, caissons, forges, all horses and harness of the artillery of the army be brought to Greensboro for disbursal.[128] In Greensboro, .54-, .58- and .69-caliber small arms and

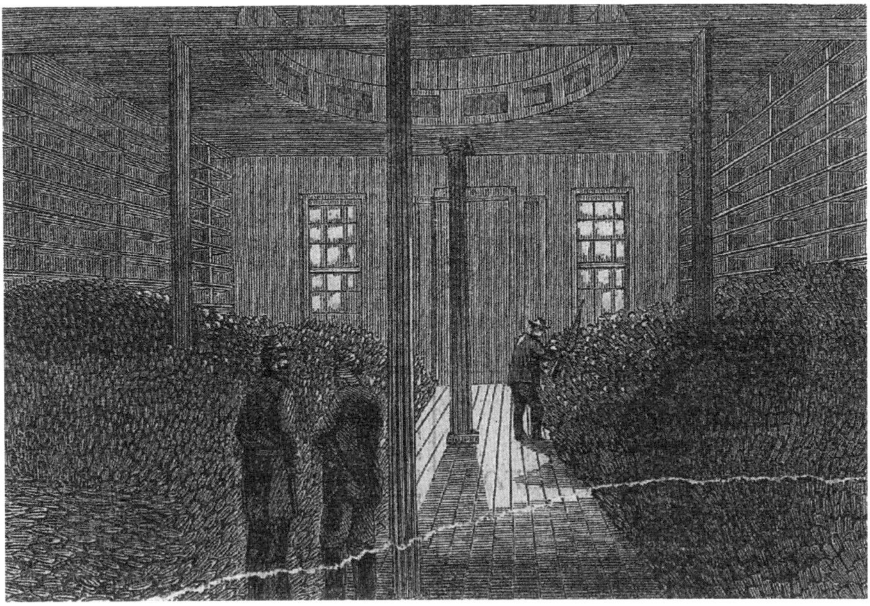

Weapons of war were gathered after the surrender of General Johnston's army. *University of Michigan Library Digital Collections.*

accompanying cartridges, accouterments, cartridge boxes, cap pouches, waist belts, bayonets, musket caps, bayonet scabbards, sabers and gun slings were deposited.[129]

In Greensboro on April 28, 1865, Governor Vance issued a proclamation calling for the people of the state of North Carolina to remain at home and conduct their business in a peaceful manner. Athos described the scene in Greensboro:

> *As April 1865 dawned upon the world Greensboro was no longer the beautiful, quiet, delightful place of yore. The streets were swimming in mud, and the houses looked as if they sympathized with their deplorable condition. "Tramp, tramp, tramp" was heard at all hours, day and night, as our infantry marched to their lines of battle. Horses and horsemen were dashing through the mud from street to street. The drum and fife and bugle were heard giving out their discordant sounds wherever a group of Confederates could be seen; and the nightly camp-fires sparkled and blazed from every hill-top and on every street in and around the town. The rumbling of passing cannons, the neighing of frightened horses, the jingling of spurs and clashing sabers, the shrill whistle of the coming engines, the tramp of the soldiery, the movement of wagons, the*

> *preparations for battle, the excitement of war and fear, the rushing to and fro of citizens and soldiers, the insubordination of desperate men, the stern mien of our veteran soldiers, the calm defiant air of our noble commanders and rulers, all presented a scene of sound and aspect never before witnessed or heard in the wild woods of this inland town, and nothing resembling it since the clash of the patriot and tory, and the stern onset and struggle of Cornwallis and Greene in the days of the Revolution which "tried men's souls."*[130]

According to Athos, General William Hartsuff of the United States Army, along with others, was the first to enter Greensboro to parole the Confederate soldiers, followed shortly by infantry, cavalry and artillery.[131] Major General Jacob D. Cox, United States Army, was in command of the Twenty-third Army Corps at Greensboro.

The wounded soldiers were removed to Edgeworth Female Seminary, and the women no longer tended to their needs but were allowed to visit with the soldiers. Mary Watson Smith recalled, "Our wounded men, sadly depleted alas in numbers, were at once transferred to Edgeworth Seminary and our occupation was gone, but we were allowed to visit them there and the old historic mansion with its beautiful ground that witnessed many glad greetings and sorrowful partings. These were the times that tried the souls of men and women."[132]

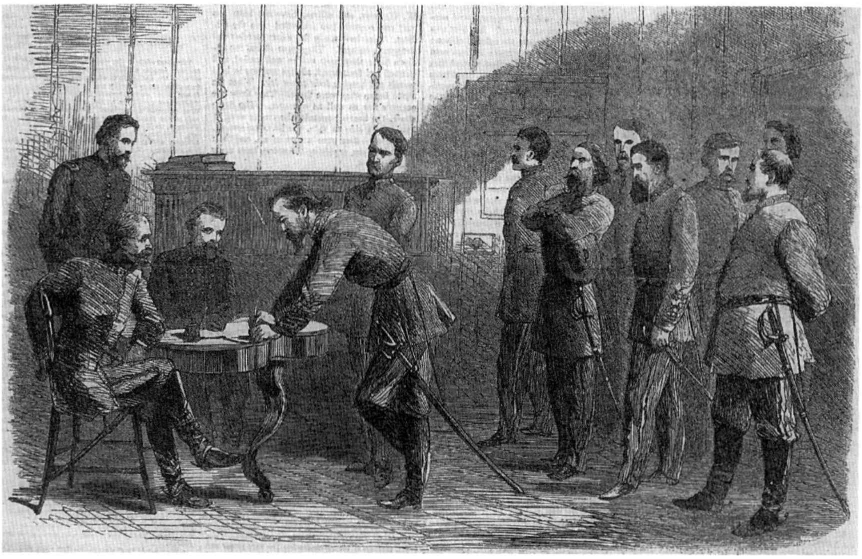

Confederate soldiers received paroles. James W. Albright was given the job of printing paroles when the supply was exhausted. *University of Michigan Library Digital Collections.*

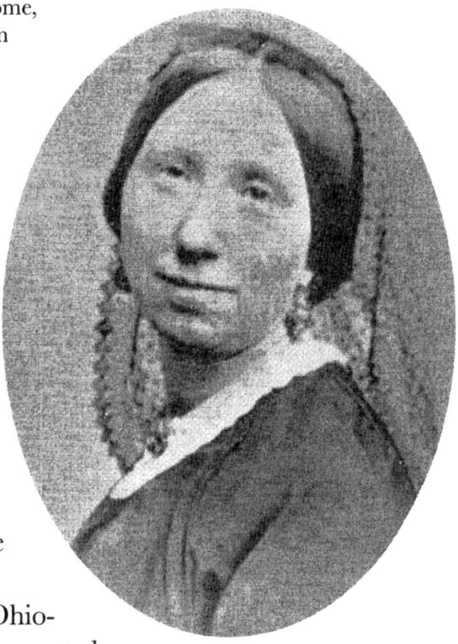

Letitia Walker recalled life at her father's home, Blandwood, during the Confederate years in a speech to the United Daughters of the Confederacy. *Bettie Caldwell.*

Women played a vital role in keeping the peace after the close of hostilities. The officers of the United States chose to occupy the largest homes in town. Blandwood, the home of John Motley Morehead, was an early choice. Morehead's daughter Letitia Morehead Walker, known for her hosting capabilities, made the intrusion as pleasant as possible for all those concerned.

Major General Cox brought his Ohio-born wife to stay with him and requested Letitia visit with his wife. Shortly, another request arrived from General Cox that he would like Letitia and Julia Gilmer to attend a review of the Northern soldiers on parade; this event occurred in June 1865. The ladies complied after being ordered to do so. A pavilion was set up in the center of the town with the upper portion reserved for the Federal ladies. Julia quite aggressively informed her husband, John Adams Gilmer, that she refused to attend. She lost the battle, and amidst tears, she complied.

Letitia wrote of the event, "Sullen, vindictive, no eulogy was paid the magnificent pageant, the gorgeous display of thousands of new uniforms, glittering sabers and bayonets, and all flushed with victory and marching to the music of splendid bands."[133] In time, however, Letitia looked more fondly on General and Mrs. Cox.

In the crowd watching the parade was an abundance of soldiers wearing the gray uniform of the Confederacy. The paroled Confederates compared their victors' precision in march and their splendid uniforms and weaponry to their own uniforms, weapons and methods of marching.

General Cox chose the beautiful home Dunleath as his place of headquarters and had his tent placed behind the house; it was the home of peace activist Robert P. Dick. Troops set up tents throughout his grounds and erected the United States flag. The family walked around the flag to avoid paying the least tribute. Mrs. Cox attempted to befriend Mrs. Dick with offerings of lemons, a treat denied the family during the war. General Cox requested that church services should continue and sent notice to Reverend Jacob Henry Smith, pastor of First Presbyterian Church.

After the service, Reverend Smith's wife, Mary, wrote in her diary, "As we passed along, every street, store, doorway and corner was crowded with federal troops, and the whole world looked blue in unison with our feelings that bitter morning. I sat throughout the service in blinding tears…lest, in sermon or prayer, some word might escape from the turbulent heart of the speaker and cause his arrest."[134]

Women also provided entertainment. Minna Raven Hildesheimer, a notable singer, often performed. At the Britton House dances entertained the soldiers. Susan Dick Weir, a talented artist and designer, created beautiful gowns for the ladies to wear from curtains. There was much private entertainment in the ladies' homes also. Lizzie Gretter (Mrs. Thomas Sloan) recalled, "Every Greensboro girl had her share of suitors." The ladies also earned income from their Northern invaders when it was discovered they paid quite well for homemade biscuits and cakes.

Guilford County's population swelled with refugees, parolees, prisoners and Confederate and United States troops. For the second time in its history, Guilford County was the scene of foraging, impressment and fear. Disillusioned Confederate soldiers tried desperately to reach their homes, and no horse or mule was safe from conscription. As Northern victors entered the county, the residents feared that assaults and murder could occur right at their front steps. Their concerns became reality in the last days of the war.

There were incidents of violence inflicted on the residents. An old man of Guilford County refused to hand over his money and was killed in Greensboro by one of Brevet Major General J. Kilpatrick's men. Kilpatrick wrote General Schofield asking if he needed to set an example and shoot the assailant, as a large portion of his command was in Greensboro with him. It was decided the man would be tried by military commission.[135]

Henry Anderson, Company D, Ninth Michigan Cavalry, was found guilty of killing Emanuel Cabel. He was sentenced to be shot to death with musketry and executed on May 13, 1865.

At the close of the war, Guilford County was overwhelmed by parolees of Appomattox, parolees of the Army of Tennessee, criminals, prisoners and deserters, all hungry and trying to fend for themselves.

A woman who went by the pen name "Luola" wrote a poem on the surrender of the Confederate army under General Johnston to General Sherman on April 29, 1865:

'Tis passed, the dream is o'er!
'Tis passed
That long and fitful dream—
That dream oft dashed with fears
But still with hope agleam:
And I awake and backward glance
On the revolving years,
Those four long years, baptized in hope
But swathed in blood and tears…
I saw our Southern troops go out
I saw their proud array;
I heard the proud defiant shouts
On many a sunny day:
I saw their pennons court the breeze,
I saw the sunlight dance
Of glittering steal and bayonet
With broken fitful glance;
And oh! How proudly did I point
To one and yet another,
And say: that is my husband—friend,
And that brave boy—my brother![136]

In Greensboro, Lieutenant Colonel R.C. Kise's 120th Regiment Indiana Volunteers command office was set up in the courthouse; J.L. Nulford, post surgeon, was at the post hospital; Captain C.S. Hall's commissary was located near the railroad on South Street; Captain Asa Teal, superintendent of the Freedman's Bureau, was located on East Street; and Captain E.W. Clarke, post quartermaster, was located on South Street immediately after the close of hostilities.[137]

Brevet Colonel T.G. Baylor, United States Army, reported conditions in Greensboro: "The number of small arms turned in is exceedingly small. This is accounted for by the utterly disorganized condition in which the troops were found. The arms are scattered throughout the country between Danville, Greensboro, Salisbury, and Charlotte, and some of them are to be found in almost every house."[138]

Weapons of war deposited at Greensboro included fifteen twelve-pounder brass guns (Howitzer); one six-pounder iron gun; one twelve-pounder mountain howitzer (brass); five twelve-pounder Napoleon guns; five three-inch wrought-iron guns, model 1861 (Rodman); two Wiard gun (steel,

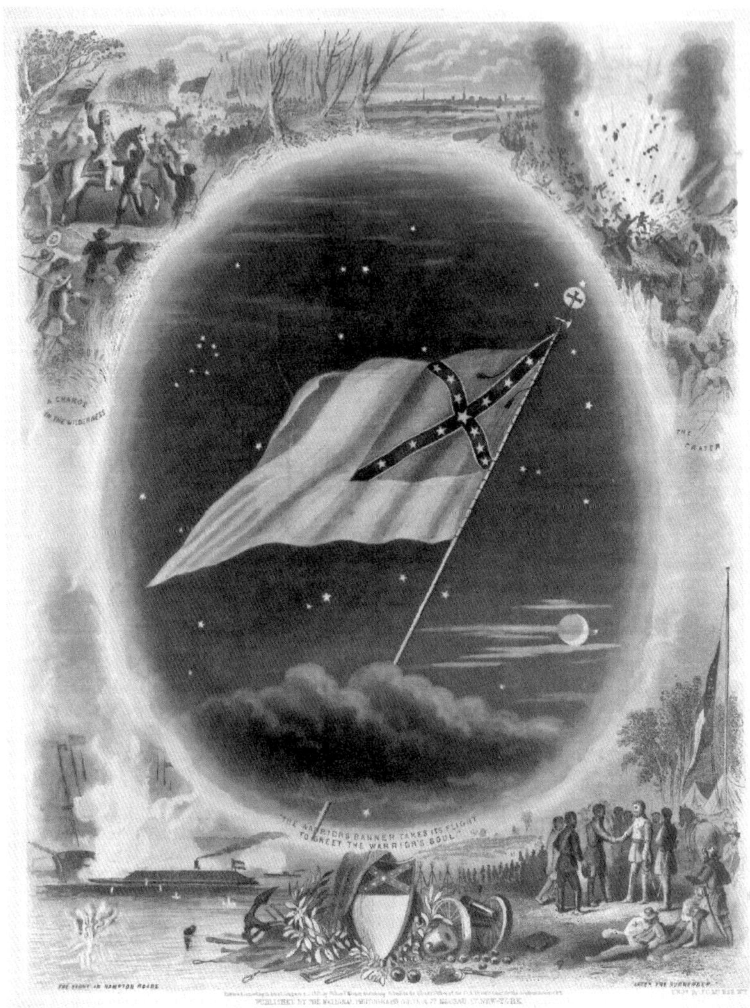

The "Stainless Banner" surrounded by battle scenes, a scene of the surrender and surrendered weapons of war. *Library of Congress.*

caliber 3.67); five six-pounder guns (brass); sixty-eight light twelve-pounder guns (brass); eleven twelve-pounder howitzers (brass); three ten-pounder Parrott rifle guns (iron); three three-inch rifles (cast iron); two twenty-pounder Parrott rifles (iron); seven six-pounder guns (brass, smooth bore); three twelve-pounder howitzers (iron); and one Brooke rifle (caliber 3.67).

Guns of foreign manufacture included two ten-pounder Whitworth rifles and two Blakely guns (caliber 4.62). United States–manufactured gun carriages included three for twelve-pounder howitzers, one for a six-pounder gun, one for a twelve-pounder mountain howitzer, five for a twelve-pounder Napoleon gun, three for a three-inch rifle gun and two for Wiard guns. In addition, 12,500 pounds of sulphur and 37,000 pounds of saltpeter were stored at Greensboro. Muskets and rifles consisted of 2,342 Springfield rifle muskets (caliber .58), 4,526 Enfield rifle muskets (caliber .577), 310 Austrian rifle muskets (caliber .58), 932 Harpers Ferry rifle muskets (caliber .58), 300 United States muskets (caliber .69), 2 Sharps carbines (caliber .52) and 3 Burnside carbines (caliber .54). Cavalry sabers numbered 130, small arms cartridges numbered 341,600 round elongated ball (caliber .58), 12,000 rounds elongated ball cartridges (caliber .54), 4,000 rounds buck and ball cartridges (caliber .69), 6,000 rounds cartridges for Sharps rifle (caliber. 52) and 500,000 percussion cups.

At Jamestown, North Carolina, two twelve-pounder heavy guns, two Napoleon guns, one six-pounder iron gun, one six-pounder bronze gun, one Dahlgren boat howitzer and one twelve-pounder iron howitzer were reported.[139] The Confederate military utilized weapons of their own manufacture, purchased weapons from foreign countries and used weapons captured from United States troops.

Officially, 39,012 paroles were issued, and 32,174 parolees received $1.17 in silver coin as final payment of their service in the Confederacy. Many of the Confederate troops simply went home once it was concluded the war was lost and did not wait for their paroles.

After hostilities ceased, the Federal soldiers were very interested in viewing the location of a great Revolutionary War battle that took place in Guilford County in 1781, the Battle of Guilford Courthouse, and rode out to visit during the summer of 1865. Armed with maps, the Federal soldiers studied the maneuvers of General Greene during the battle and compared their own tactics with those used by Greene.

Northern entrepreneurs, often referred to as carpetbaggers, arrived in Guilford County, set up businesses, bought land and started factories. Albion Winegar Tourgee (1838–1905), a Union veteran, settled in Greensboro. Tourgee fought at the Battle of Manassas, was captured at the Battle of Perryville and participated in the Battle of Chickamauga before leaving the United States service due to a back injury. He was openly hostile toward the Southerners and was very active in politics. He organized the Loyal Reconstruction Leagues and promoted the rights of newly freed slaves and all people of color.[140]

At war's end, Addison Coffin, previously active with the Underground Railroad, assisted many Quakers in their move from the area, while

Quakers from other parts of the country attempted to stop the departures and aid those still in Guilford County. There was such an exodus from Guilford County that it was feared the county would lose its entire Quaker population if procedures were not enacted to stop the exodus. Much-needed supplies—food, clothing, shoes and hats—were sent to the Guilford County Quakers who had endured years of shortages.

The Baltimore Association of Friends to Advise and Assist Friends in the Southern States formed in 1865 and worked hard to revive the Friends' meetings and schools. The group also worked with English, New England and Philadelphia Friends to establish a Freedman's Association.

To counteract the westward migration, the Friends purchased a farm they named Swarthmore Farm in 1867 to promote improved agricultural practices. The purpose was to teach Quakers and others better farming techniques and to stop the migration from Guilford County. The farm was quickly renamed Model Farm and was a success. The farmhouse still stands in High Point and is on the National Register of Historic Places.

The Thirteenth Amendment to the Constitution abolished slavery; it was ratified on December 6, 1865. Thus began a new life for those who were once bound in slavery's chains.

Many young men from Guilford County took part in the western migration in the United States after the war. Their war losses were great, and the West was seen as a new beginning.

Artificial limb programs helped disabled veterans. In Guilford County, many veterans took part in the program to acquire artificial arms and legs. During the war, amputation was viewed as the only course of action for certain wounds, and many a veteran not only suffered the loss of a limb but also pain his entire life as a result of war wounds. Some, however, had even greater losses: many a woman in Guilford County continued her life after the war a widow.

Slowly, the nation started the long process of healing that continues today.

Chapter 7

Warnersville

The recently freed slaves—already left homeless and penniless after the war—were uprooted once again by fears of disease. Smallpox threatened the area, and the "Negro" camp was afflicted.[141] The camp remained until the last week in March 1866, when it was abolished. Disabled freedmen were sent to a camp at Salisbury, North Carolina; it wasn't recorded where the healthy freedmen were sent.[142]

Some of the freed children were taken in by white families to work as apprentices and learn a trade. Still others worked for their former masters as servants and lived in the household with them. Some of the former slaves were bequeathed an inheritance upon the deaths of their former masters. Many freed slaves left their rural homes and flocked to larger communities in hopes of creating better lives in areas with established Freedmen's Bureaus.

The Association of Friends of Philadelphia and Its Vicinity for the Relief of Colored Freedmen, a Quaker group, determined to help the recently freed slaves in Guilford County and elsewhere. One member, Yardley Warner, came to Greensboro from Pennsylvania and lived among the free persons of color and the recently freed slaves. Thirty-five and a half acres were divided into lots of about one acre so that each family had enough ground to cultivate a garden. The land, previously owned by Hugh Rice, was sold on December 5, 1865. A second parcel consisting of one and a half acres was purchased on May 28, 1866, from James M. Garrett.

The subdivision was named Warnersville in honor of Yardley Warner. Harmon Unthank, a former slave, became a leader in the community and was often referred to as "the boss." He built a large house on McCullogh Street. An English Friend, Henry Stanley Newman, visited Warnersville and asked the name of the community. Unthank thought about it, and the next day asked a teacher to paint in large letters the word "Warnersville" on a board, which he promptly attached to a post at the schoolhouse.

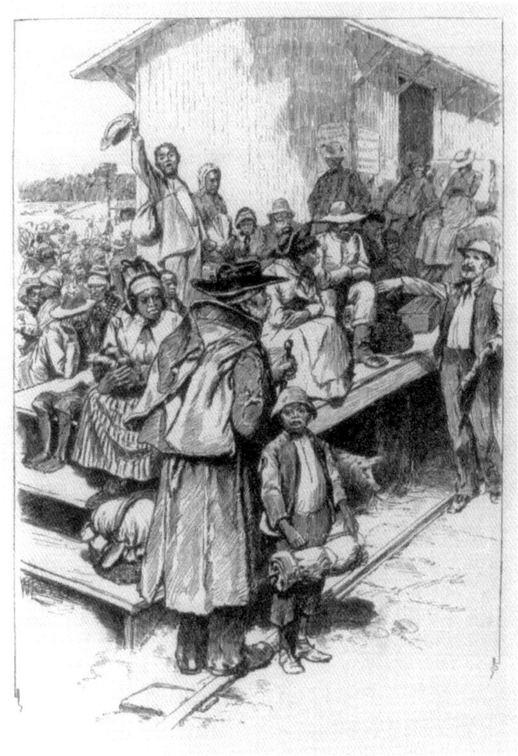

Some freed people chose to leave rural areas for opportunities in towns and other states, while others remained with their former owners. *Library of Congress.*

Newman spoke of some of the early teachers, George and Emmie Dixon and Miss Swinborne, of England. The teachers stayed at a mission house on the property. The schoolhouse stood on the corner of Ashe and McCullogh Streets. A student, Hannah Payne, recalled that the white women lived on Ashe Street. At first, many of the students were sent away to attain a better education at schools such as Hampton Institute. Afterward, they returned to teach at Warnersville. Newman relates that the pastor, Reverend R.C. Campbell, prayed for the Society of Friends, saying, "O Lord, they stood by us in the hour of our sorrow and distress and difficulty: do Thou, dear lord, stand by them now, and prosper them in all their efforts. They helped and taught us when we did not know what to do; do Thou help them and give them good success in all they are doing throughout the world for the welfare of their fellowman."[143]

Nicholas Moody moved his family from Surry County in 1872 to become residents of Warnersville. Yancey Gibson; Harmon Unthank and his son Jasper; James Jones, a Methodist preacher; Mangum Walker; and Grace McLean also each bought a lot. Later, McLean married Anderson Nelson, a teacher who taught in a school that eventually became known as J.C. Price School. Allen Hairston, Jack Gorrell, Solomon Williams, Orpheus McAdoo, Lillian Cummings, Thomas Jackson, Jonathan W. McAdoo, Alfred Adams, Constantine Davie, Charles Albright, James Howell, Charlotte Gibson, Washington Gorrell, Matt Weatherly, Lydia Thompson and Albert Keiser also resided in Warnersville.[144]

Friends established smaller projects in the Guilford townships of Friendship, Oak Ridge and Jamestown. Warner taught a school in the African American community called Little Davie in an area known then as Bush Hill. Warner died in Bush Hill, North Carolina, on January 4, 1885, of typhoid fever. Bush Hill is today's Archdale and is situated in Guilford and Randolph Counties. A school was established in High Point for the benefit of the recently freed slaves.

After the war, a migration of Northern men arrived in Guilford County. The Union officers and other Northerners settling in Guilford County and other parts of the South are often referred to as carpetbaggers. A carpetbagger was one who wished to profit from the spoils of war. Several men of the Warnersville community worked twelve-hour shifts as carpenters in a spoke and handle factory operated by former Federal soldiers McMann and Crane. The men of Warnersville found jobs as porters, general laborers, carpenters, firemen, shoemakers, waiters and dishwashers.

Women of Warnersville working outside the home were limited in their job opportunities. Some went on to be teachers, but the majority of the women were in service jobs such as maid, nurse, cook or washerwoman. Many of the jobs were in the homes of white people, and the pay was menial. Mrs. L.E. Bailey ran a boardinghouse on Davie Street, opposite the railroad. Due to segregation, it was nearly impossible for a traveling African American to find a place to stay.

The early residents of Warnersville suffered from a lack of medical care. Their diseases—the same as those of their white counterparts, such as measles, typhoid, whooping cough, pneumonia and tuberculosis, to name a few—took their toll. Approximately 60 percent of the people buried in Union Cemetery (an African American burial ground) were dead before the age of twelve. Slowly, medical care became available as residents Drs. Cordice and Stewart opened a hospital for African Americans in 1914.[145]

St. Leo's Hospital opened in 1906 and accepted all patients regardless of race or religion. L. Richardson Memorial Hospital, founded in 1927, was formerly the Greensboro Negro Hospital. Lunsford Richardson, founder of Vicks VapoRub and other remedies, supported the hospital to the point that it became a top-rate facility.

Warnersville, to the south of Greensboro, became a culture within a culture—a culture of African Americans living parallel but separate lives from their white counterparts. They developed their own businesses, including grocery stores, restaurants, barbershops, night clubs and even a funeral home. The social climate still dictated that many work for white business owners and perform services for white households. St. Phillip AME Zion Church was established in 1866.

Warnersville has survived the passage of time and is still a viable African American community despite the fact that urban renewal in the 1960s almost destroyed the community. Many African American businesses were destroyed before an opportunity to move to another section of the community was available. Physical remnants from the past remaining are the J.C. Price School and Union Cemetery. Descendants of slaves and free persons of color still reside in Warnersville. In many cases, documentation of early historic communities such as Warnersville is only possible through reading the old hand-carved marble monuments in the cemetery, as records were not kept or, if kept, were lost over time.

Union Cemetery was listed on the National Register of Historic Places in 1993. The cemetery, established by 1880, is located at South Elm and East Whittington Streets. It consists of about four acres and is the first public cemetery in the community for African Americans. The need for a cemetery for African Americans was great because segregation of the races did not end at death. Three churches—St. Mathews Methodist and Providence Baptist, both established in 1866, and St. James Presbyterian, founded in 1867—united to provide a burial ground for their membership and African Americans in general. It is not known when the first burial occurred, but Hiram Lindsay, an African American, was in charge of Union Cemetery in 1880 and until his death in 1918. Lindsay is buried in Maplewood Cemetery, established in 1917 for African Americans. When Maplewood Cemetery opened, burials in Union Cemetery gradually ceased. There are graves of former slaves, though most of the individuals buried in Union Cemetery were born after the end of the Civil War in 1865. The number of individuals buried there is not known definitively, though evidence suggests over 1,025 burials. Of that number, only 115 of those have grave markers, though there are many sunken areas denoting graves. Prior to the opening of Union Cemetery, African American burials occurred in rural areas of Guilford County and near the cemeteries of traditional white churches.

Sarah McKenzie (1829–1914) served the Warnersville community as a midwife, delivering over five hundred babies. "Aunt" Jane Sloan (1843–1910)

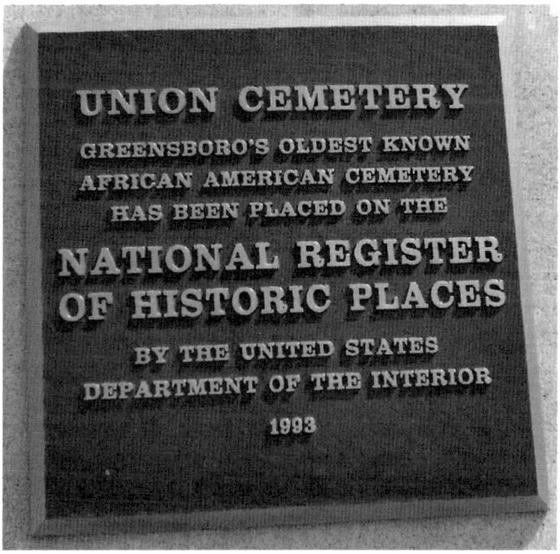

Union Cemetery was established by three churches to provide a burial ground for African Americans, some of whom were former slaves. *Author's collection.*

was a nursemaid to the short story writer O. Henry. Sloan and McKenzie are buried in Union Cemetery and believed to be former slaves.

In an unmarked grave, according to tradition, rests Harmon Unthank, the one-time boss of Warnersville who decided to name the settlement after Yardley Warner. Unthank was born a slave and rose to be a leader of society with an interest in everything that advanced humankind. Unthank was a member of the county school board and on the board of directors for the People's Five Cent Savings Bank, a first for an African American in the South.[146] Unthank became a close friend to Judge Albion Tourgee, a former Union Civil War officer.

Reverend Mathew Alston (1821–1884), founding member of St. Mathews United Methodist Church in 1866, was supposedly one of the fictional characters in Albion Tourgee's *Bricks Without Straw.* Alston's feet turned inward, and Tourgee's character Eliab Hill bears a striking resemblance to Alston. Alston's burial location in Union Cemetery is marked with a tombstone.

There are many individuals born of slave parents interred there. William (Willie) Logan, son of enslaved Pocahontas (Polkie) Logan, was born shortly after the war and thus born free. His mother and brother Warren were slaves of the Smith family in Greensboro. Warren, after freedom, graduated from Hampton Institute and served as a teacher at Tuskegee Institute, quickly becoming treasurer and principal and thus proving the profound effect education had on the former slaves. On his military application, William was described as having a yellow complexion, gray eyes and black hair and was 131 pounds and five feet, seven and a half inches tall. He enlisted in 1898 as chief musician of the Third North Carolina Colored Volunteer Infantry. It was the first infantry regiment entirely manned by those of African American descent. Mimicking the flag presentations of the 1860s, the African American women of the community bestowed on Company D of the regiment a silk flag. Though it was decades after the Civil War and the men were a part of the military to protect the United States, this group was subjected to horrible discrimination. Descendants of slaves buried in Union Cemetery served in the western part of the United States as Buffalo Soldiers and in the Spanish-American War and World War 1.

Research is lacking regarding service in the military during the Civil War, though it is known that John Gilmer, described as "colored," was listed on the roster of the Guilford Grays, Twenty-seventh North Carolina, Company B. Gilmer left Guilford County sometime after the war, and he received a Confederate pension. The Guilford Grays' roster before the war listed Jake Mebane, fifer; Bob Hargrove, kettle-drummer; and Caesar Lindsay, base-drummer, all three considered to be African Americans and probable slaves as their names do not appear on any United States census records. According to a death certificate, a Caesar Lindsay who died in 1911 is interred in Union Cemetery. Research is lacking, but it is highly probable the Caesar Lindsay of the Guilford Gray militia is the same one buried in Union Cemetery. Bob Hargrove has at least one child buried in Union Cemetery, though no indication exists of his own burial there. Often, the surviving family members didn't know the deceased parents' names or the birth locations of the deceased; often if born in slavery and sold, the individuals had no memory of their ancestry or the locations of their birth.

Several of the white men to go to war from Guilford County joined the ranks and took their body servants (African American, free or slave) with them. The body servants were often childhood friends, and in many cases, great bonds existed between the masters and their slave servants.

For example, Captain John A. Sloan Twenty-seventh North Carolina, Company B, had his bodyguard, Bill, with him, and after the battle in March 1862 at Newbern, North Carolina, Bill left him and "held his ground" until the train reached Greensboro. Bill says he simply went home to inform "mar's Robert that mar's John was safe and untouched." According to Sloan, "He [Bill] returned in due season and enlisted with [Sloan] durin' the war, was faithful to the end, and is part of our history."[147]

David J. (Jarvis) Gilmer, a son of former slaves Madison and Caroline Gilmer, rose in military rank to captain of the Third North Carolina Colored Volunteer Infantry while stationed at Fort Macon, North Carolina. He erected a monument in honor of his parents at Union Cemetery and had a letter he wrote carved in the stone: "To my Father and Mother, Madison and Caroline Gilmer: I never knew my mother.

She died during my infancy. My father was a friend to an honest man. I never knew him to tell a lie or abuse a neighbor. David J. Gilmer."[148]

The wording on the old marble stone is no longer readable. David J. Gilmer is buried in Maplewood Cemetery in Greensboro.

A portion of a letter written on July 7, 1920, by David J. Gilmer to members of First Presbyterian Church of Greensboro when he donated funds to go toward the building of their fourth church building states:

> *My mother, though a slave, was, I am told, a member of the Presbyterian Church of which you are now a member, and from there she became a charter member of St. James Presbyterian Church, which I understand, was set apart for the colored members of your church who were members of it at the close of the Civil War. I was born a Presbyterian and was christened in St. James, but my mother having died before I was old enough to know her, I became a ward of the Methodist Church and Bennett College and, from that environment became a Methodist, identified with St. Mathews Church here, where I now belong.*[149]

The First Presbyterian Church was established in 1824, with eight white members and four slaves: Tony; Milly and Molly, slaves of Reverend Paisley; and Kezia, a slave of Robert Carson.[150] From its founding, the church offered religious services to free persons of color and slaves. After the Civil War, the church started a Sabbath school for the freedmen and assisted them when they decided to establish their own church, St. James Presbyterian Church, which exists today.

Free persons of color residing in Guilford County in the area that became Warnersville included James (1834–1902) and his wife, Lucinda Mitchell Dean (1834–1911), described as mulatto in the 1850 Guilford County Federal Census. In 1860, on the eve of the Civil War, the Dean family was living next door to Zepherriah and Bettie Mitchell, both described as mulatto. James and Lucinda Dean are buried in Union Cemetery. James was a brick mason who owned his own business.

Carved in marble stone in Union Cemetery are the surnames Lindsay, Morehead, Holt, Jones, Logan, Lyles, McAdoo, McClintock, McConnell, Donnell, Mendenhall, Sloan, Smith, Wharton, Dillard, Dick, Scales and others—identical surnames of their former masters who are buried in similar but segregated historic white cemeteries.

The citizens of Warnersville faced many hardships—including lack of medical care, inadequate nutrition, racial prejudices, attempts at disenfranchisement, Jim Crow laws and segregation—but they persevered, and the community continues to flourish in the twenty-first century. One young man raised in Warnersville, Ezell Blair Jr. (Jibreel Khazan), is remembered as one of the "Greensboro Four" who sat down at a "white's only" counter and refused to give up their seats at Woolworth's in Greensboro on February 1, 1960. Today, the Woolworth building is home to the International Civil Rights Center and Museum.[151]

The Civil War may have ended in 1865, but for many in Guilford County, the emotional and personal impact spanned generations.

Chapter 8

Memorial and Heritage Organizations

The work of the Soldiers' Aid Society ended with the final days of the Confederacy. Women's work, though, continues until the present day. Immediately after the war, ladies' memorial associations formed throughout the South. The Ladies' Memorial Association in Greensboro was established on May 11, 1866. The ladies gathered at the courthouse with plans to cherish the memory of the unknown Confederate dead and preserve their graves.[152]

Mary Winn Gretter, president; Mrs. W.F. Fontaine and Mary Watson Smith, vice-presidents; Julia Gilmer Glenn, treasurer; Letitia H. Morehead Walker, corresponding secretary; and Mrs. Sterling, recording secretary, were the first officers. Managers were Mrs. Charles Potts, Mrs. Robert Paine Dick, Mrs. Boles, Mrs. Dickson, Mrs. W.P. Hughes, Mrs. Levi Marshall Scott, Mrs. Robert W. Lindsay, Mrs. John Sloan, Mrs. Brenizer, Sabre Long, Virginia Bilbro, Mary Gorrell, Sallie Fontaine and Emma Troy.[153] The society printed a notice in the local paper that read, "Resolved that all persons who make donations for the purpose of carrying out the objects of the said society shall be considered members of the society, and that their names be registered in a book kept for that purpose."[154]

During the war years, women attempted to meet the needs of their loved ones as they fought for Southern independence. After the war, the women attempted to give dignity to the dead by providing them a decent Christian burial. In many ways, women were exhibiting their continued patriotism of the Lost Cause with their dedication to memorializing Confederate dead. The burial of the Confederate dead was met with hostility, in some cases, by the victors who recalled their comrades and relatives killed in battle. It was easier for the women to initiate memorial work because everyone understood the heartache of a mother who had lost a son in the horrid war. It was quite another case for former Confederate soldiers to honor their war dead, as it was frowned upon by the victors. After military rule ended in North Carolina in 1868, men took a more active role in memorial work.

The Confederate dead were scattered throughout the county, alongside railways and roadways. The bodies were gathered and placed in a mass grave south of Greensboro; a similar gathering of the dead occurred in High Point. The Ladies Memorial Society oversaw the removal of the dead in Greensboro. Men assisted with the digging of the mass grave and the reburial of the dead.

In time, the ladies became sickened by the condition of the mass grave in Greensboro that held the remains of 234 men, and an organization was established in 1869: the Greensboro Eclectic Literary Club. The group consisted of Confederate veterans, daughters of the original Soldiers' Aid Society and wives and children of Confederate veterans. Members included John Staples, P.F. Duffy, Mary Campbell, Charlie Gorrell, Miss Eckel, Lottie Gretter, W.A. Horney, M.L. Lindsay, Annie Lindsay, J. Morehead Jr., Sue Scott, W.C. Porter, Eugene Morehead, J. Chase Gilmer, Annie W. Long, Davie Gretter, Sallie Greene, John A. Gilmer, S.L. Gilmer, Mary Strayhorn, R.G. Glenn, P.H. Adams, Hattie Adams, Josie E. Scott, Minnie Foster, Murray Smith, R.M. Hill, James M. Morehead, W.E. Benbow, Mattie M. Sloan, Lizzie Gretter, Lula Lindsay, Lewis C. Howlett, Mike Gretter and several others whose names are lost to history. Eugene Morehead was president; Samuel Smith was secretary. The club was active in raising funds to finance memorial objectives. Concerts and plays were organized, and practice sessions turned into social occasions. The Greensboro Eclectic Literary Club consisted of male and female members who worked together on similar objectives, one of which was to maintain the graves of those who died during the war. In reading the history of this club, one can assume it had been very private about its memorial work.

In a letter from S.C. Caldwell to her cousin Bettie D. Caldwell, librarian at the Greensboro Public Library, Caldwell states that after she left Greensboro, the club undertook the care of Confederate graves. She seems to think that Joseph Morehead collected the bodies of Confederate dead and placed them in a cemetery.[155]

Though literary in nature, the Greensboro Eclectic Literary Club took on the task of removing the nameless Confederate dead from their mass grave and moving them to a new Confederate Cemetery located adjacent

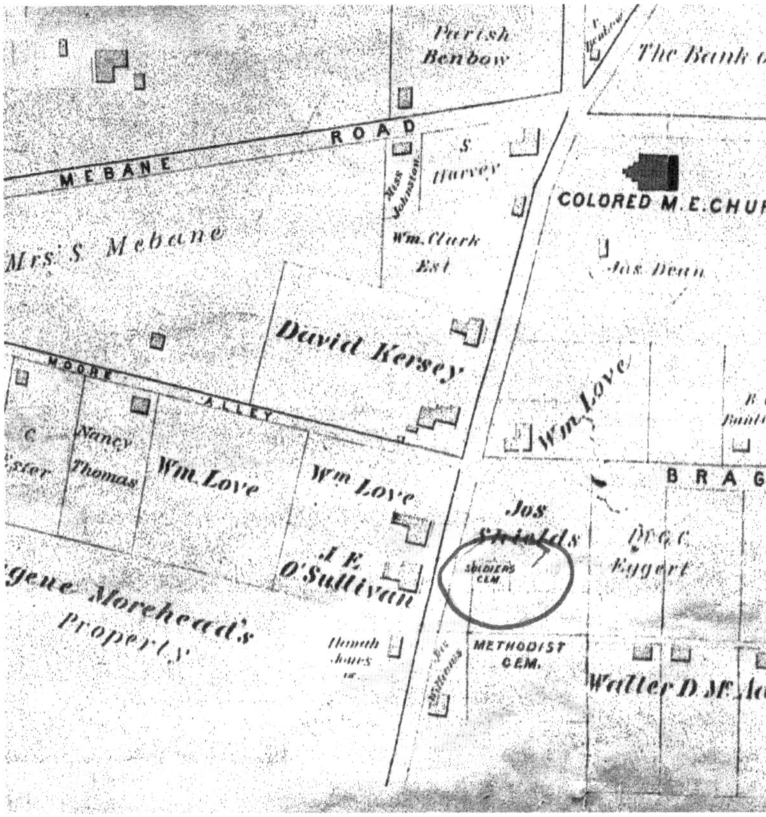

This map shows the location of the Confederate Cemetery, adjoining the Old Methodist Cemetery before both cemeteries were removed to Green Hill Cemetery. *Greensboro Public Library.*

to the Methodist Cemetery (the Methodist Cemetery was moved to Green Hill Cemetery in 1917), south of Bragg Street and east of Mebane Street in Greensboro, so the graves could be better maintained.

The first publicly known record of a Decoration Day in Greensboro was in 1870. In time, Decoration Day became known as Confederate Memorial Day and is held in Guilford County and throughout North Carolina annually on May 10. An article in the local paper described the event that occurred on May 6, 1870:

> *"Furl that banner sadly, slowly! Treat it gently, it is holy."*
> *At 10 AM, according to previous notification, those who had not forgotten the sleeping dust of those who died for us, assembled at the Court House*

> *with floral offerings. Hence the procession—formed two and two—went to the new Confederate Cemetary* [sic]*—purchased by the Greensboro Eclectic Literary Club. This spot adjoins the Methodist graveyard and is neatly fenced with nice white palings. The bodies were removed from their old resting place, near Warnersville, last winter, by the Club and re-interred, where they may be protected and cared for. Two hundred and thirty four solders,* nameless *all but four, here sleep the sleep that knows no breaking.*[156]

Supposedly, of the 234 soldiers, only 4 were identified, and today, even those 4 are unknown. Reverend Mangum of the Methodist Church gave the speech at the cemetery on May 6, 1870, saying, "The good knights are dust, and their swords are rust and their souls are with the saints we trust."[157] Sisters, brothers and friends decorated the known Confederate graves in the Methodist and Presbyterian cemeteries in Greensboro also. It was hoped a monument could be erected over the dead eventually.

Reverend Mangum said, "Bring flowers to deck each patriot grave, and bless the vernal sod, where sleep those fallen ones, whose deeds are written with their God."[158]

Later on in the evening, the Greensboro Eclectic Literary Club celebrated its first anniversary. John N. Staples, a member of the club and a Confederate veteran, was the orator, and a large group attended the meeting.[159]

The following year, on May 6, 1871, wartime peace activist and anti-secessionist Robert P. Dick was the orator. Addressing the group, he said:

> *We have met here today to place our offerings upon the graves of some of these noble men. They were strangers to us all and died far from the sorrowing, weeping loved ones at home; but kind hands closed their dying eyes and placed them in this hallowed spot. I may have differed from many of them in political feeling and sentiment, but I can respect their opinions, admire their courage, and honor them as heroes. I cannot regard them as rebels and traitors for they were my noble and glorious countrymen. As the representative of the Eclectic Club, as a North Carolinian, and as a patriotic citizen of the Great Republic, I now place this memorial wreath of flower and evergreens upon these greatest of our country's children and heroes. It is an ephemeral offering, for it will soon be withered and dead, but I trust that admiration for the generous, noble and brave will never die, but be as immortal as the principles of justice, virtue and truth, and that for many generations to come, the patriotic citizens of this great nation, forgetting all sectional strife and entertaining for each other the*

> *warm and generous feelings of brotherhood, will annually assemble and place tributes of affectionate remembrance upon all of the graves of their heroic countrymen.*[160]

On May 3, 1872, former North Carolina governor and Confederate veteran Zebulon Vance delivered the Memorial Day address. Vance said:

> *It is our duty, the duty of those for whom they died, to keep alive the memories of their nobleness and unavailing courage…It is our duty to keep fresh and green the record of their deeds, and when in calmer times the muse of history takes up the pen to write the story of their ill-fated struggle, she may find abundant material, replete with truth and justice…Then I can but commend this custom of annually honoring the graves of our fallen heroes. Care for the dead has been in all ages a good test of civilization. It is redolent not only of the most beautiful humanity but is especially suggestive of the immortality of the soul and of that great Christian doctrine of the resurrection when the bodies of these our slaughtered children shall arise in glorious array, even as the flowers have arisen from the earth, clothed with beauty such as can only be bestowed by him whose hand paints the lilies of the valley and adorns with its wondrous tints the rose of Sharon.*[161]

In 1873, at the Confederate cemetery, Judge John Alexander Gilmer, former colonel of the Twenty-seventh North Carolina, delivered the memorial address:

> *Fully assured that, in every true Southern heart the recurrence of this day brings back crowded memories that are sad, grief's* [sic] *that are holy, and affections that are dear, to allow you to suppose that I hastily and with no reluctance assume drawing from these sacred fountains thoughts for public presentation today would be untrue to this occasion and unjust to myself. I would therefore speak discreetly and tread softly, here, o'er the lowly mounds and in the presence of these dead.*[162]

In 1876, Junius Irving Scales, a Confederate veteran, was the keynote speaker, and he said:

> *In a forcible, nervous style, with just enough historical reminiscence to be interesting, he referred to the origin of the war, showing the three causes that led to the failure of the Confederacy, the blockade of her forts, the superior wealth, and above all the overwhelming numbers of the North, one side, enlisting*

> *foreign troops in her aid, contending for the preservation of the Union—the other pouring forth the flower of her chivalry, from every gentle house in our fair Southland, to battle for State sovereignty, nobly contending for principles bequeathed us by the first great rebel, Washington, himself. Life after life, the pride, strength and joy of fair homes, was quenched in battle, until from hall and cottage, throughout the length and breadth of our darkened land rose the burden of the tearful ballad, "The flowers of the forest are a' fa'en away."*[163]

Interestingly, the Fourth of July was celebrated again in Guilford County in 1876 after a sixteen-year lapse. The last celebration before the war occurred in 1860, when a monument was erected at Alamance Presbyterian Church Cemetery for Colonel Arthur Forbis, who was killed in battle at Guilford Courthouse in 1781.[164]

Over a decade after the war, Guilford County residents were still grieving, or so a newspaper article insinuated during the Fourth of July event. "Everything passed off pleasantly and was very interesting considering it is usual on such occasions to have a military display."[165]

Memorial Days in Guilford County were very elaborate events, and businesses and schools closed. Early in the day, amid drumrolls, the people met at the courthouse in Greensboro armed with floral tributes. They formed a parade consisting of various organizations, such as the City Band, the Greensboro Fire Company, the International Order of Odd Fellows, choirs from multiple churches, the Ladies' Memorial Association, Confederate veterans and schoolchildren. When the veterans could no longer walk in the parade to the cemetery, they were taken in buggies and, later, motor vehicles. Poems were read, songs sang and massive amounts of flowers placed upon the graves.

After the 1876 celebration, the *Greensboro Patriot* printed the following tribute:

> *And over their dust the fresh tears fell, of a nations' holy grief.*
> *With sable-draped banners, and slow measured tread.*
> *The flower-laden ranks pass the gate of the dead,*
> *And, seeking each grave where a comrade's form rests,*
> *Leave tear-bedewed garlands to bloom on his breast.*
> *The flowers of the forest are a' fa'en away.*[166]

Confederate Memorial Day in 1879 is of interest, as it indicates Federal veterans were involved in the proceedings, as evidence by this report from the *Greensboro Daily News*: "Order of Procession: Greensboro Brass Band; Fire Company; Odd Fellows; Good Templars; city and county officers; the orator of the day and chaplain; the Ladies' Memorial Association; soldiers of the late war, Federal and Confederate; officers and pupils of the Greensboro Female College; Sunday schools; citizens."[167]

In 1884, the Ladies' Memorial Association oversaw the removal of Confederate dead from the Confederate Cemetery adjoining the Methodist Cemetery. It was reported, "The mayor and commissioners of Greensboro donated a memorial square in Green Hill Cemetery for the purpose. The ladies plan to raise funds to erect an appropriate monument. Until funds are raised plans are to plant grass and shrubs to beautify the mound."[168]

A committee of Confederate veterans removed the Confederate dead to Green Hill Cemetery. According to Annette Sloan Tinsley (granddaughter of Mary Winn Gretter, president of the first Ladies' Memorial Association in Guilford County) in her newspaper article "Greensboro's First Memorial Day," "The writer remembers a simple funeral march from the Methodist Cemetery to the city [Green Hill] cemetery where the bodies were placed in a central mound."

In 1888, the Ladies' Memorial Association ordered a life-size figure of a Confederate soldier made of copper to place on a base in Green Hill Cemetery. "The cost is 350 dollars, delivered in the city—which amount the ladies have; but a granite or marble die will cost about 100 dollars additional, which the ladies will ask the citizen to contribute. The statue will not reach Greensboro by May 10th, hence no formal celebration will be held at this time."[169]

Amid delays, the Confederate Memorial Monument at Green Hill Cemetery was finally unveiled, and according to the inscription on the monument, the event occurred on June 3, 1888.[170] The inscription, "Our Confederate dead 1861–1865 dedicated to the memory of 300 unknown soldiers by the Ladies' Memorial Asso. [Association] of Greensboro, NC" was added at some point in the history of the monument. The former burial location of the additional 66 unknown soldiers is not recorded, but they were reburied with the 234 who died as a result of the battle at Bentonville, North Carolina, that occurred March 19–21, 1865, for a total of 300 soldiers.

Guilford Battleground Company invited all Confederate veterans to unite with the veterans of Guilford County in celebration in 1893: "No present party affiliations affect in any way the brotherhood of the survivors of the Lost Cause; they are now as true and loyal to the government established by their forefathers as they were to the Confederate States, for which they so bravely fought and suffered."[171]

The United Confederate Veterans (UCV) Guilford Camp 795 organized at the courthouse in Greensboro on October 5, 1896, with J.W. Scott serving as commander and T.J. Sloan as adjutant.

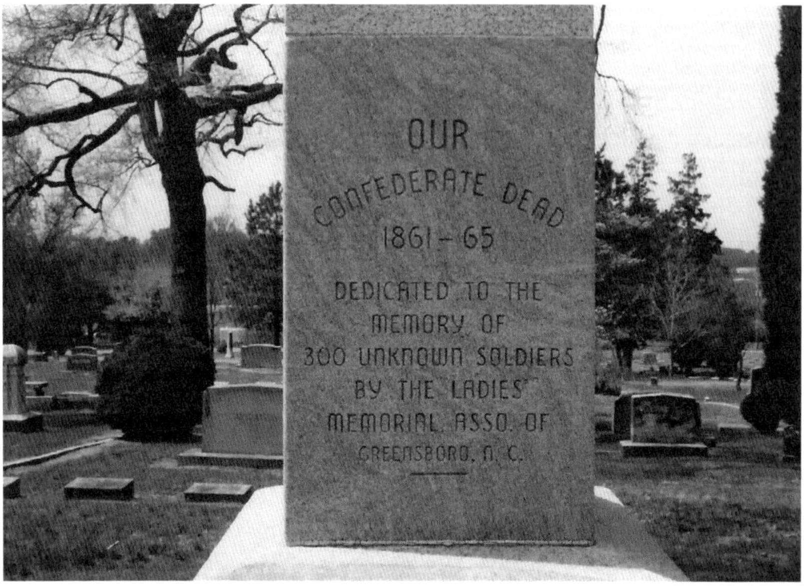

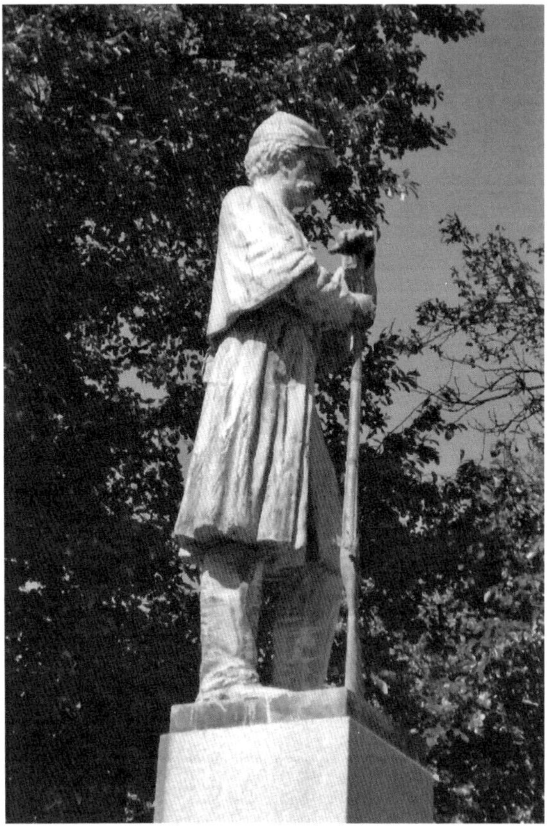

Above: A portion of the Confederate monument at Green Hill Cemetery relating the dedication of the Ladies' Memorial Association to the unknown soldiers. *Author's collection.*

Left: The bronze Confederate statue ordered by the Ladies' Memorial Association cost $300, including delivery to Greensboro. *Author's collection.*

Guilford Chapter 301, United Daughters of the Confederacy (UDC), was chartered on April 27, 1899, with the following officers: Caroline Fowle Sparrow Dalton, president; Ella Preston Burch Brodnax, first vice-president; Sallie Lindsay Gilmer, second vice-president; Anne Elizabeth Porter Caxton, recording secretary; Augusta Harrison Allen, corresponding secretary; Charlotte J. Gorrell, treasurer; Lucie Bevens Schenck; Maude Harris Brooks; and Annie E. Gorrell. Lucy Robertson, president of the Battle Abbey Association, was made an honorary member.

The early members of Guilford Chapter 301 were outstanding members of the community. Member Sallie Walker Stockard was the first woman to graduate from the University of North Carolina in 1898. She was an author and published a history on Guilford County as well as other publications. Her father and brothers fought for the Confederacy.

Many of the charter members of Guilford Chapter 301 were also members of the Ladies' Memorial Association, so the work of honoring the Confederate dead continued in Guilford County and the care of the Confederate monument became the work of Guilford Chapter 301. A Northern woman who married a Confederate veteran could become a member, but she could not hold office in the organization.

In High Point on a rainy July 4, 1899, a monument to the memory of the Confederate dead in the Oakwood Municipal Cemetery was unveiled. General J.S. Carr and F.C. Robbins delivered the address to a large crowd. Professor G.H. Crowell, superintendent of High Point graded schools, presented the monument.[172] W.R. Lowdermilk was master of ceremonies. Helen Snow, Mary English, Hattie Sechrest, Zelma Purnell and Vera Idol unveiled the monument, which was erected by the Junior Order of Mechanics.[173] At the conclusion of the ceremony, a banquet was held with over eight hundred people in attendance. Mr. Burnett traveled from Charleston, South Carolina, to be in attendance and brought with him a floral decoration from the Daughters of the Confederacy in Charleston.[174] Burnett's brother, Captain Burgh Burnett, First South Carolina Infantry, Company F, has an existing monument located near the Confederate monument. Dead soldiers' bodies were gathered from various areas in the High Point vicinity in the years after the war. Wording carved on the fifty grave monuments tells the story of suffering and death.

Fred Hilburn, Third Mississippi—whose name is on a list dated April 28, 1865, at General Hospital 12 in Greensboro, where he was paroled—is one of the fifty buried near the Confederate monument in High Point. Two

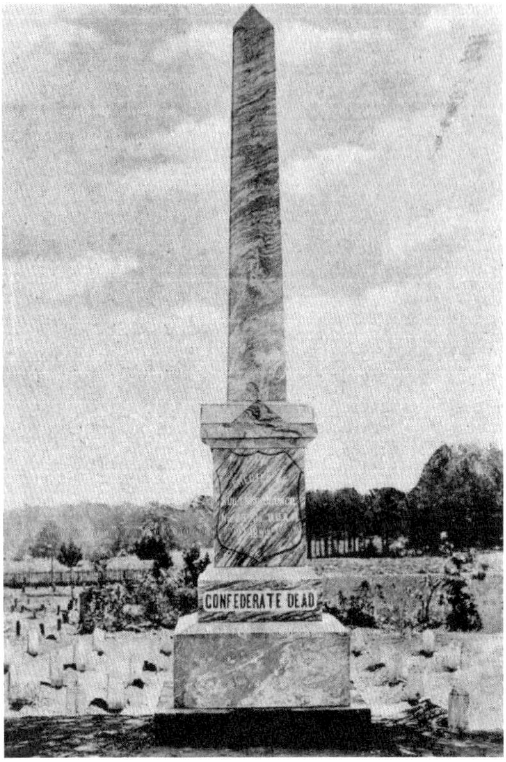

Left: High Point Confederate Monument was erected in Oakwood Municipal Cemetery, High Point, by the Junior Order of Mechanics in 1899. *North Carolina Collection, Wilson Library.*

Below: A monument adorned with an iron Southern Cross of Honor directs the way to the graves of fifty Confederate soldiers in Oakwood Municipal Cemetery. *Author's collection.*

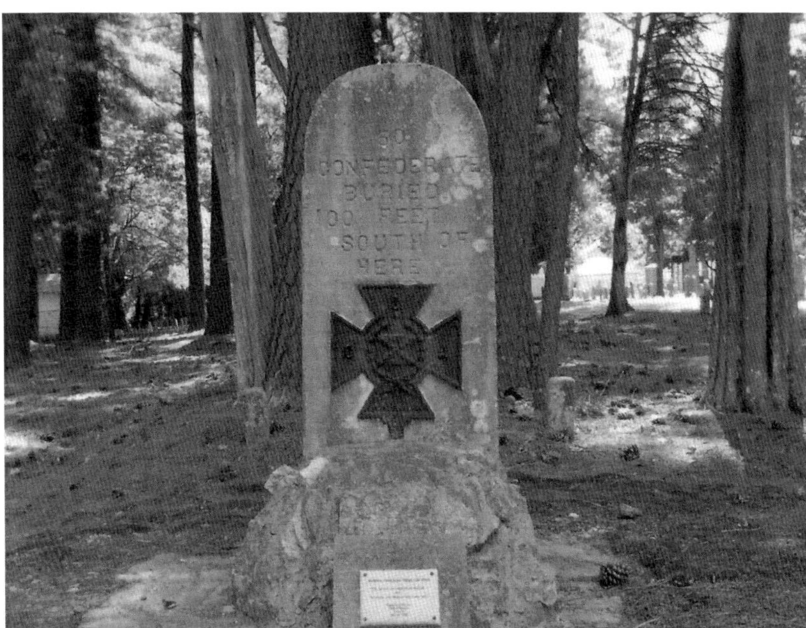

others—Peter Cunningham, Thirty-second Georgia, Company D, and C.F. Bell, Twentieth Alabama, Company A—were at CSA (Confederate States of America) Hospital 3 in Greensboro preceding their deaths. A few of the fifty soldiers buried in Oakwood Municipal Cemetery appear to have been admitted to hospitals in Greensboro prior to receiving medical treatment at High Point. Oates Sutton, Forty-sixth North Carolina, Company I, was last reported in April 1865 in Raleigh suffering with paralysis, and evidently he was loaded on a train toward Greensboro. George Arwood, Forty-second North Carolina, Company D, was reported on May 1, 1865, at a hospital in Greensboro. Sutton and Arwood are also numbered among the fifty buried at High Point. Due to the aged conditions of the soldiers' grave markers and inscriptions with various misspellings, it is difficult to document their travels before their deaths in High Point. Two monuments are carved with the word "Unknown," and others have the states from which the soldiers enlisted—Alabama, Tennessee, Louisiana, Florida, Georgia, South Carolina, North Carolina and Mississippi. These men from throughout the South and far from family found their final resting place in the soil of Guilford County.

On October 29, 1906, a High Point chapter of the Daughters of the Confederacy, 1036, was established with Mrs. J.B. Richardson as president.[175] The chapter no longer exists. Memorial events at the High Point monument continue annually.

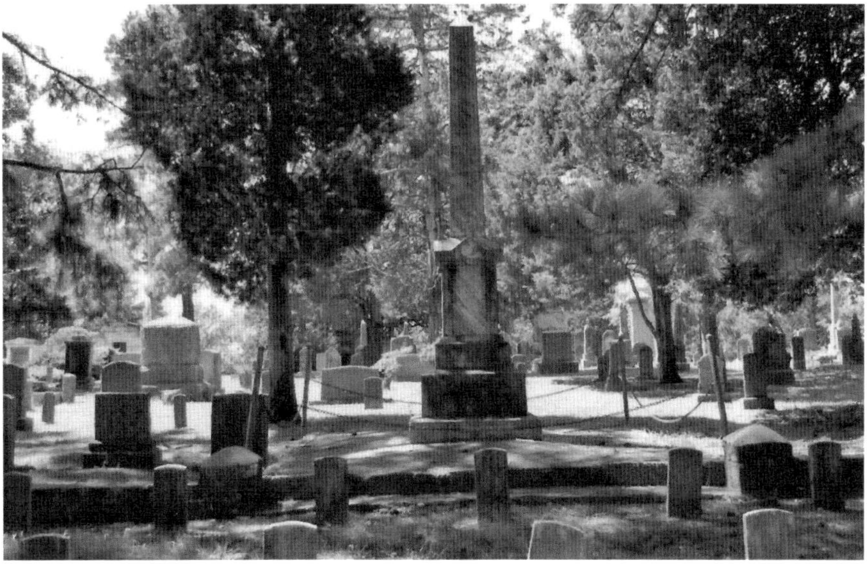

The Confederate monument at Oakwood Municipal Cemetery has the colors of the Confederacy painted on its base. *Author's collection.*

At Green Hill Cemetery on Confederate Memorial Day on May 10, 1901, the orator was General Matt W. Ransom, who spoke for an hour and a half. The *Greensboro Patriot* reported a portion of what was spoken:

> *The noble daughters of the South have written and are writing the most beautiful page in all history. If all the orators, all the poets and all the statesmen of all times had combined their genius to pay tribute to the dead, what tribute more tender and touching could have been devised than this, on the 10th of May, bringing sweet offerings of spring, to the altars of the dead? Better than marble and brass are these offerings from the heart. There is nothing in the history of the action of the Confederate soldiers to bring a blush to your cheeks. They deserved a greater triumph than the Romans ever had.*[176]

Confederate Memorial Day in Greensboro, fifty years after the end of the war, began after the annual meeting of Guilford Camp 795, United Confederate Veterans, which was held at the courthouse. The veterans and the United Daughters of the Confederacy traveled in cars to Green Hill Cemetery. Young girls wore Confederate colors and sang. The veterans formed a circle around the monument and covered the mound with flowers. A male quartet sang "Tenting on the Old Campground Tonight." Reverend Alexander D. Betts said the benediction. Afterward, the veterans were taken to Smith Memorial building for dinner served to them by Guilford Chapter 301, United Daughters of the Confederacy. They enjoyed fried chicken, ham, pickles, coffee, cake and ice cream. The Daughters handed out chewing tobacco, smoking tobacco and pipes. Dr. Melton Clark, chaplain of Guilford Camp 795, United Confederate Veterans, made a few remarks and closed his address with a song titled "We Are Old-Time Confederates" to the tune of "Old-Time Religion."[177]

Sanford Kirkpatrick, a Union war veteran, regularly attended the meetings of the United Confederate Veterans and was beloved because of an incident in the war and his efforts to assist both the Union and Confederate veterans. While he was a Representative in the United States Congress, he attempted to get a bill passed to take the veterans of the District of Columbia to Gettysburg for a reunion. Captain John Hickey, a Confederate veteran, began a conversation with Representative Kirkpatrick and was interrupted by the congressman, who said, "Your voice seems familiar to me. Were you at Corinth?"

Hickey replied, "Yes, that is where I lost my arm and leg." The conversation continued, and Kirkpatrick asked Hickey, "Do you recall a Yank who found you on the field, bleeding in the thickest of the fight?"

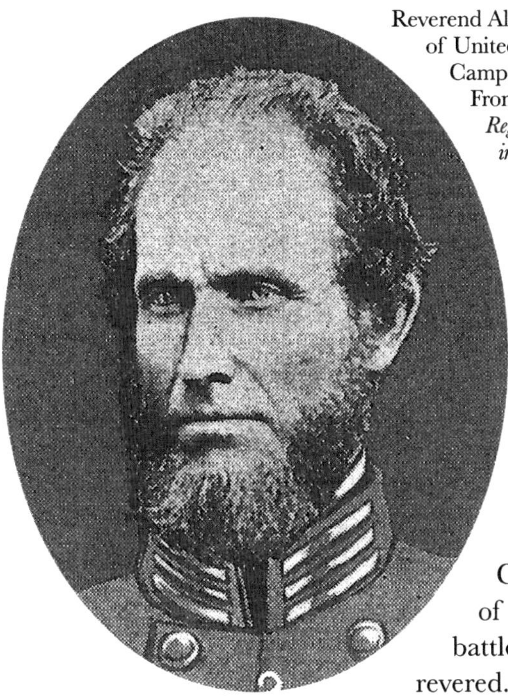

Reverend Alexander Betts served as chaplain of United Confederate Veterans, Guilford Camp; he is buried in Green Hill Cemetery. From Walter Clark's *Histories of the Several Regiments and Battalions from North Carolina in the Great War 1861–1865, Written by Members of Their Respective Commands.*

Captain Hickey excitedly replied, "Are you that Yank? Are you the boy who gave me a drink from his canteen, patched up my wounds and dragged me to safety?"[178] Once the Confederate veterans learned of this benevolent act on the battlefield, Kirkpatrick was revered. When Kirkpatrick moved to Greensboro, he was welcomed by the United Confederate Veterans, Guilford Camp 795. He took an active part in the events attended by the Confederate veterans.

On May 10, 1916, flowers were twined about the Confederate monument at Green Hill Cemetery. The veterans attended the ceremony as honor guards. The old vets reminisced about the many battles they participated in while doing their duty. The program began at 10:30 a.m., but instead of the old custom of marching to the cemetery, many people furnished automobiles so all could ride from the courthouse to Green Hill Cemetery. The Confederate monument was surrounded by as many as five hundred people. Little girls helped decorate with flowers and sang patriotic music. The address was delivered by J.H. Bennett. Reverend Betts gave a short talk, led the group in the singing of a song about meeting on the other side of the river and finished with a prayer. Afterward, the group traveled in automobiles to W.D. McAdoo's property to enjoy a barbecue supper. After supper, Reverend Melton Clark, pastor of First Presbyterian Church and chaplain of the Greensboro camp of veterans, spoke. It was mainly a farewell address from the reverend, as he was moving to Charleston, South Carolina.[179]

The Laura Wesson Chapter, UDC, organized in 1928 and consisted of younger women. The chapter was named in remembrance of the young woman

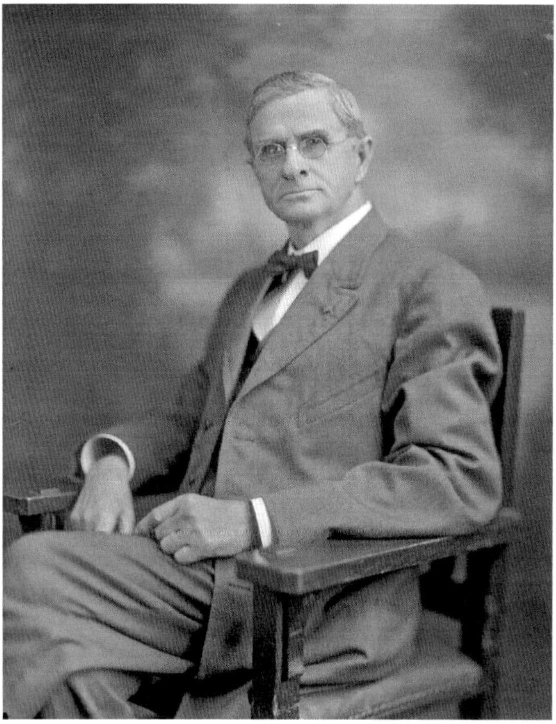

Left: Sanford Kirkpatrick served in the Second Iowa Infantry, United States Army, and was welcome at United Confederate Veteran functions in Guilford County. *Library of Congress.*

Below: Union and Confederate veterans stand in front of a banner honoring the Tar Heel State, "First at Bethel and Last at Appomattox." *Library of Congress.*

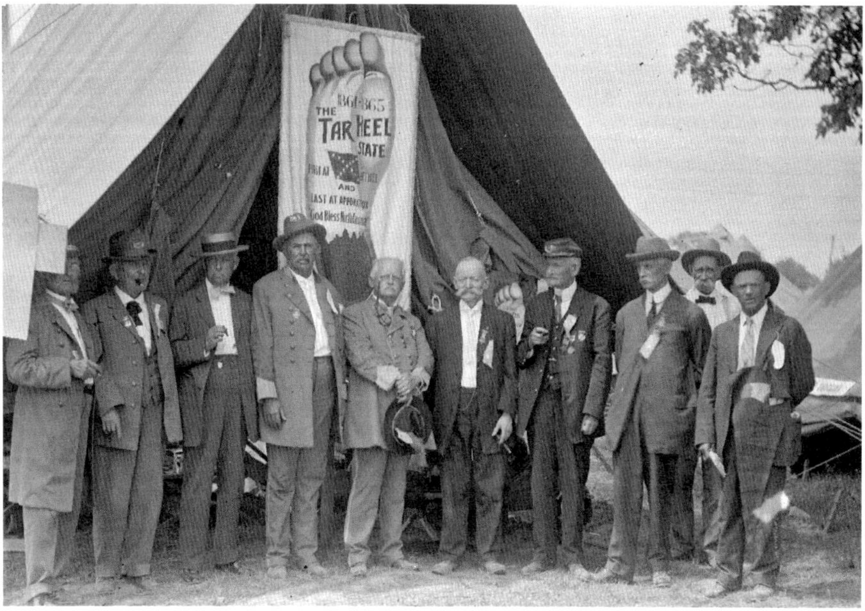

who stood steadfast and nursed the sick soldiers suffering with smallpox at High Point before eventually succumbing to the disease herself. She is buried at Oakwood Municipal Cemetery, and a memorial marker in her honor is located near the fifty soldiers who died at the Confederate hospital there.

In 1930 in Greensboro, eighteen Confederate veterans were on hand for the ceremony. The *Greensboro Daily News* reported: "With gray heads bared and with tears in dimming eyes the little band listened to the inspiring words of Reverend H. Grady Hardin at the monument to the Confederate dead."[180]

Reverend Hardin addressed the veterans, saying, "To you noble men of gray who live as our inspiration do we today pledge the best we have to follow in your footsteps. We love you and shall always love you and try to bring comfort and joy to the evening days of your lives. May the sunset be more glorious than you have ever dreamed and may it turn into a more glorious dawn than this world has ever known."[181]

The veterans decorated the base of the memorial with flowers the children had handed them earlier. The tribute was also for beloved general Robert E. Lee. The monument was garlanded with oak leaves and decorated by Guilford Chapter 301, UDC. The grave of every Confederate soldier was decorated with a Confederate flag. As the veterans left, they were given smokes and candies,[182] and Lizzie Lindsay ended the session with a farewell. Lindsay exhibited Southern patriotism throughout her life. When just a child during the war, she was a member of the Children's Soldiers' Aid Society. She served as president, Guilford Chapter 301, United Daughters of the Confederacy, during the years 1913 to 1927.

After speeches at the courthouse in 1935, four Confederate veterans led the way to pay respects to the Confederate dead. Guilford Chapter 301, UDC, arranged a luncheon afterward. The United Confederate Veterans organization ceased to exist as the old veterans passed away. G.H. Grantham, a member of Guilford Camp 795, UCV, died in 1937, the last known member in the community.[183]

To observe Memorial Day in 1940, the Greensboro Historical Museum put on display 327 sermons preached by Reverend Jacob Henry Smith (nicknamed the "Rebel Parson") during the war. At the First Presbyterian Cemetery a plaque titled "To the Soldier Dead" was unveiled honoring the military dead interred there. J. Lathrop Morehead of the Presbyterian Graveyard Association was in charge of the unveiling. Guilford Chapter 301, UDC, handled the first part of the ceremony. Robert F. Mosely presented the address.[184]

In the 1940s, two college auxiliary chapters of the UDC formed, one at Woman's College at Greensboro (now University of North Carolina–

Greensboro) and one at Greensboro College. These chapters no longer exist. The Annie B. Daniel Chapter 2118 was established in Greensboro in 1941. The chapter was named in honor of Mrs. Garland Daniel, an honorary division president. It was very active in assisting the war effort during the Second World War until war demanded the women go to work in jobs traditionally held by men and the chapter became inactive.

In 1969, the Confederate statue placed above the Confederate dead in Green Hill Cemetery suffered vandalism. The gun held by the copper soldier was broken off and taken. Elihu Weaver Camp 1290, Sons of Confederate Veterans, repaired the monument.[185] In 1984, John Sloan Camp 1290, Sons of Confederate Veterans, restored the monument and added a granite section to raise the monument.

In 1992, Lieutenant F.C. Frazier Camp 668, Sons of Confederate Veterans, organized in High Point. The camp was named in honor of Felix Cicero Frazier.

On November 17, 2007, Guilford Chapter 301, UDC, added an inscription to the monument: "Which became the Daughters of the Confederacy, Guilford Chapter, 301, 1899." The additional inscription was to increase awareness that the memorial work of the Ladies' Memorial Association was bequeathed to Guilford Chapter 301. A small group of mostly chapter members attended the dedication.

On May 10, 2008, the Great Seal of the Confederacy mounted to the shaft of the Confederate Memorial Monument was dedicated.

Also in 2008, a large tree limb fell during a windstorm and struck the copper soldier, causing severe damage to the monument. The John Sloan Camp 1290, SCV, was in charge of the restoration of "Old Reb."

On May 10, 2011, 150 years after the beginning of the war, at precisely 6:00 p.m., at Green Hill Cemetery, Confederate Memorial Day began with a prayer titled "Call to Remember." The Honor Guard posted Southern flags and the United States flag. Lizzie Lindsay Chapter 776, Children of the Confederacy, placed a wreath at the mound. The Honor Guard performed an honor salute. Guilford Chapter 301, UDC, added a protective and decorative wall to protect the Confederate monument at Green Hill Cemetery. Confederate Memorial Day 2011 was an enchanting memorial service orchestrated by President Joanne Phipps Sharpe, Guilford Chapter 301, UDC. Toward the end of the service, twilight was darkening the memorial grounds, creating an intoxicating glimpse back in time. Keynote speaker Carol Moore stated, "To stand at the memorial and know that Confederate veterans once stood on the same ground, members of the United Confederate Veterans 795 once stood

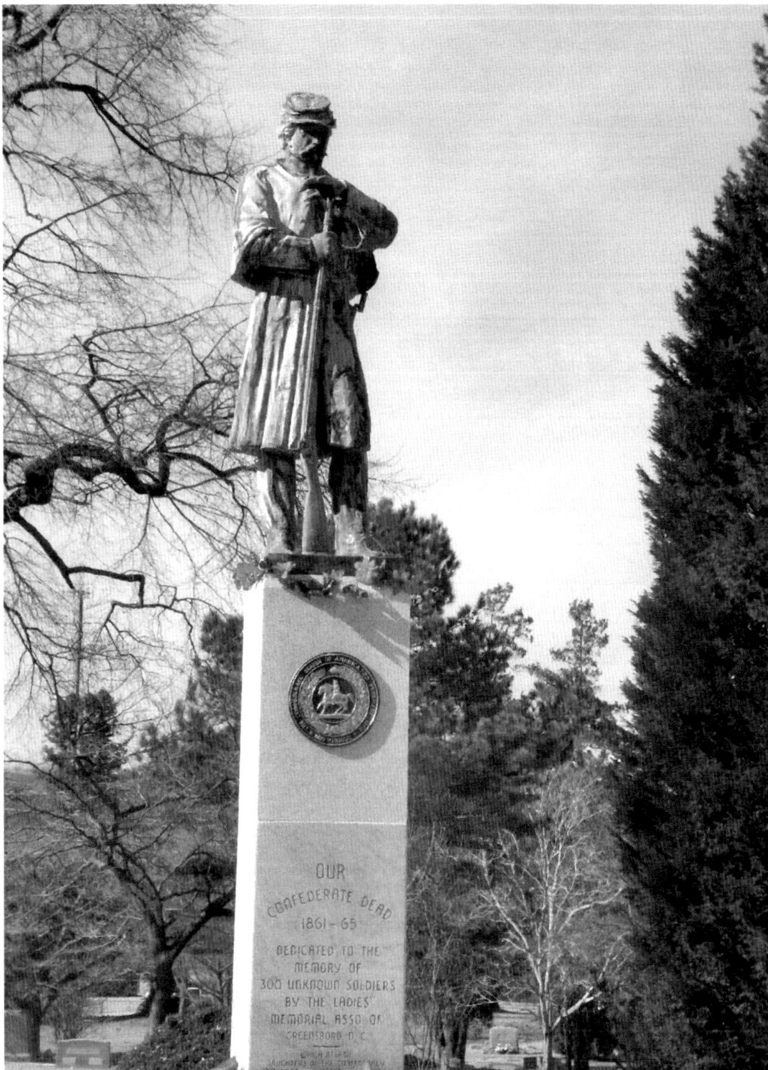

The Confederate monument at Green Hill Cemetery showing the Seal of the Confederate States of America is decorated for the holidays. *Author's collection.*

on the same ground, ladies of the Ladies Memorial Association once stood on the same ground, and charter members of the Daughters of the Confederacy, Guilford Chapter 301 once stood on the same ground makes the location truly wonderful and mysterious, a place where the past meets the present meets the future." At the end of the ceremony, everyone sang "Dixie."[186]

In 2015, the final year of the sesquicentennial of the Civil War, the Children of the Confederacy, Lizzie Lindsay Chapter and the Burke Davis Chapter, will present the Memorial Day program. It is desired the children have a leading role during the final year of the sesquicentennial, as they are the future of the UDC and SCV.

The ladies' associations in Guilford County have evolved and withstood the test of time, and their work continues in the form of Guilford Chapter 301, UDC. The women of the various soldiers' aid societies, ladies' memorial associations and Daughters of the Confederacy have bequeathed their work to their descendants, who continue the work of preserving and honoring the memory of the Confederate veterans and all veterans forward throughout time.

The Order of the Confederate Rose was named in honor of Rose O'Neal Greenhow, notable Confederate spy. The Order of Confederate Rose consists of men and women, though not necessarily descendants of those who served in Confederate service. The Mary Harper Morehead Chapter 11 is named in honor of the May queen of 1860 who presented the flag to the Guilford Grays. The Laura Wesson Chapter 5, High Point, is named in honor of the young woman who nursed the Confederate soldiers suffering with smallpox until the disease killed her. Mattie Clyburn Rice was a member of the Laura Wesson Chapter. Miss Mattie, as she was affectionately addressed, was a "real" daughter of Confederate veteran Weary Clyburn, a slave at the time of his service to the Confederacy. The term "real" is used to differentiate between actual daughters of Confederate veterans and female descendants generations removed. Miss Mattie was also a member of Guilford Chapter 301, UDC; she died in 2014.

Various memorial and heritage organizations have existed in Guilford County throughout the generations. The Military Order of the Stars and Bars (MOSB) was founded in 1938 in Columbia, South Carolina. Garnet-Pettigrew Chapter 67, MOSB, is active in Guilford County. Members descend from officers and civil officials who served during the war. Their pledge states: "We the posterity of the Officer Corps and civil officials of the Confederacy, do pledge ourselves to commemorate and honor the service of the leadership these men rendered in the cause of the fundamental American principles of self-determination and states' rights and to perpetuate the true history of their deeds for the edification of ourselves, our society, and for generations yet unborn."[187]

Conclusion

Few physical remnants of the war exist in Guilford County. An exception is Blandwood, former home of John Motley Morehead and now a house museum. The Weir home, an antebellum house, is the current home of the Greensboro Woman's Club. The railroad bed of the Piedmont Railroad at Reedy Fork, where President Davis passed moments before its destruction, can still be located, though it is endangered. A few farmhouses from the era still stand in the county, though most of the history related to the homes is now lost to time. Though the original structures may be gone, wayside signage is scattered throughout Guilford County to explain what once happened during the war.

Confederate memory still exists in the hearts of the descendants of the Confederate men and women who struggled through the "late unpleasantness." The Lowrey family of Oak Ridge sent four sons off to war to fight for the Confederacy. James Addison Lowrey survived and returned home minus a leg, but his brothers were not so fortunate. William Jahaney Lowrey died on the second day of fighting at Gettysburg, Pennsylvania; Hugh White Lowrey died on March 7, 1865, having been in the hospital at Greensboro; and John Robert Lowrey went off to war, but after 1864, he was never heard from again. Their cousin James Gray Lowrey was shot in the head and died in a Richmond hospital in 1864. He is buried in Old Union Graveyard, Oak Ridge. When the Lowrey brothers went off to war, they left their recently widowed mother and four young siblings at the homeplace.[188]

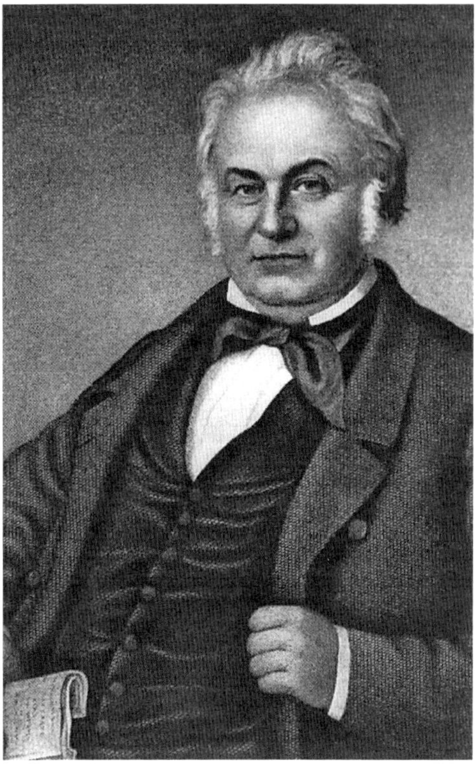

John Motley Morehead served as a member of the Confederate Congress. He is better known as the "Father of the North Carolina Railroad." From Burton Alva Konkle's *John Motley Morehead and the Development of North Carolina 1796–1866.*

Historic churchyards and cemeteries throughout Guilford County contain Confederate graves. It is as if each grave is a chapter in a huge volume telling the story of the war that pitted brothers against brothers. The First Presbyterian Church Cemetery holds the remains of three members of the Confederate Congress—John Motley Morehead, John Adams Gilmer and James Robert McLean—and numerous soldiers. James Robert McLean served the First Confederate Congress from 1862 to 1864.

The heartache of losing so many sons to the Lost Cause resulted in their names being spoken often throughout history: "[The people of Guilford County who attended the peace meetings] thought no doubt of Adams, Cole, Charles, Gorrell, Weatherly, and Weir—the young and the brave, who had gone down to bloody graves, in defense of the holy 'soil of Guilford.'"[189]

The names of these young men have been repeated often when telling the story of Guilford County during the War Between the States. Captain William Adams's gravestone at Green Hill Cemetery states he was killed while leading a charge at Sharpsburg, Maryland, on September 17, 1862. Carved on the stone are his last words, "Leave me and fight on, let me die on the field" and the words, "He has fought his last battle, for his country he died but his memory shall live." Lieutenant Colonel Christopher Columbus Cole's fallen monument was originally in the old Methodist Cemetery, which was removed to Greenhill Cemetery, and tells his story carved in stone: "[He] was killed leading the 22nd N.C. Regiment at Chancellorsville, May 3, 1863."

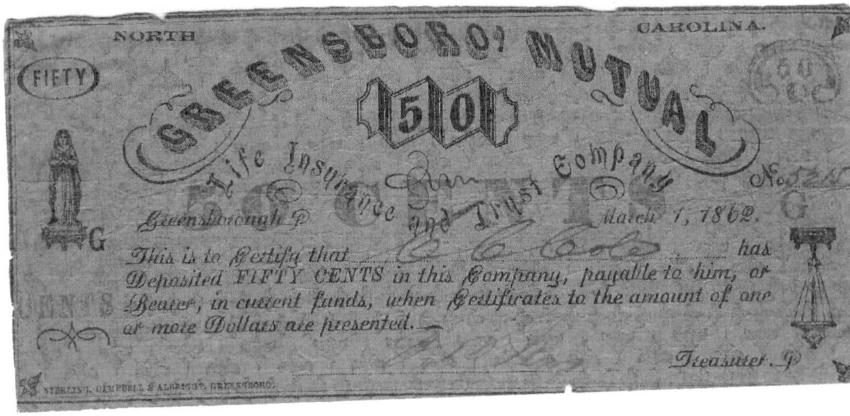

Greensboro Mutual Life Insurance and Trust Company note, printed by Sterling, Campbell and Albright, was payable to C.C. Cole, killed in battle. *Author's collection.*

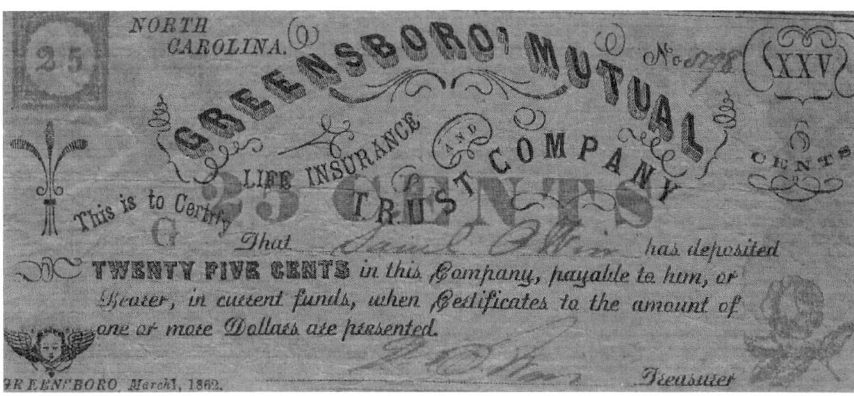

Twenty-five-cent note, dated March 1, 1862, payable to Samuel P. Weir, killed in battle at Fredericksburg, Virginia, on December 13, 1862. *Author's collection.*

Captain Harper Evans Charles, a former student at Oak Ridge Institute who taught in the schools of Guilford County before the war, lost his life at Fraser's Farm on June 30, 1862, part of the Seven Days Campaign. Etched on his aging marble monument are the words, "Slain in Confederate Service." Captain Henry Clay Gorrell's epitaph states, "Killed in battle, June 26, 1862." He was shot dead through the forehead. Sergeant Major Robert Dudley Weatherly died from wounds received in battle at Bristow Station, Virginia, in October 1863. Carved on his marble monument in First Presbyterian Church Cemetery: "Soldier, rest! Thy warfare o'er.

Sleep the sleep that knows not breaking, dream of battlefields no more." Second Lieutenant Samuel Park Weir's epitaph states that he was "killed at Fredericksburg." Weir was shot through the left temple while urging wounded friend Colonel John Alexander Gilmer to leave the battlefield.

Throughout Guilford County, the cemeteries with their old marble monuments silently tell the story of the war between brothers. Lieutenant Colonel William Henry Chapman, Forty-third Battalion (Mosby's Battalion), Virginia Cavalry, is buried in Green Hill Cemetery. Lieutenant Colonel William Chapman Society, North Carolina Military Roundtable is active in Guilford County; its purpose is to encourage the teaching of the history of the United States and its military in a fair and impartial manner. Marian T. Chaplin's monument, moved from the Old Methodist Cemetery to Green Hill Cemetery in 1917, has his story carved in stone telling of his birth in Beaufort, South Carolina; his military service in the Beaufort Volunteers; and his death on May 19, 1865, in Greensboro.

After the war, Brigadier General Alford Moore Scales, from neighboring Rockingham County, served in the United States Congress, served as

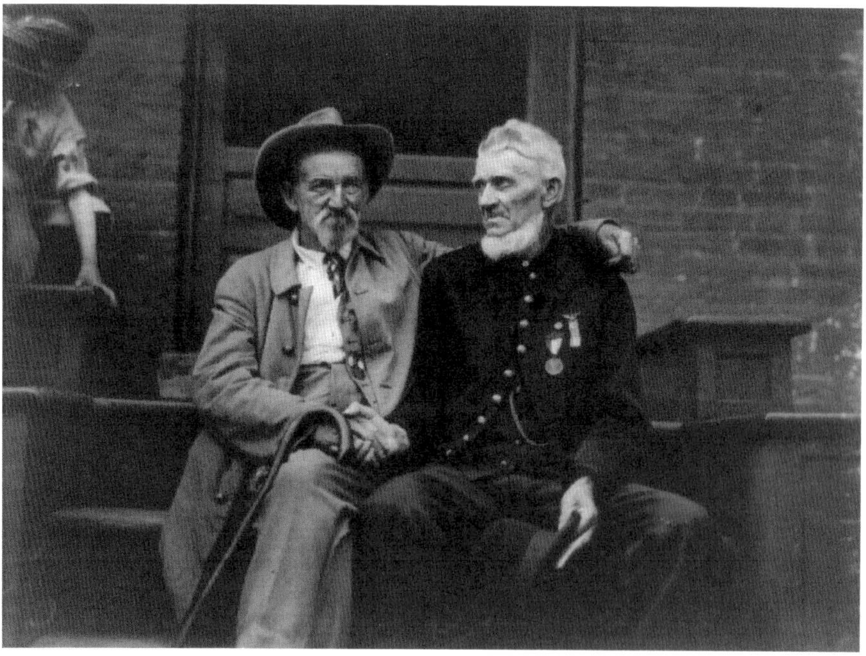

Soldiers who once wore the blue and gray and fought one another united after the war in a common cause: their country. *Library of Congress.*

governor of North Carolina and resided in Guilford County. He is buried in Greensboro's Green Hill Cemetery.

As needs arise, memorial and patriotic societies form to protect and keep repaired the Confederate graves in Guilford County. They disband when the work is completed and trust the next generation to stand guard over the memories and graves of those who once wore the gray.

Nearly 150 years after the war, reenactors don uniforms of both the North and South and reenact battles and camp life with precision, and floral remembrances are still placed on the graves of those who wore the blue and the gray. Even now, there is a strong Southern remembrance in Guilford County that transcends time and continues through the generations. To this day and always, the people of Guilford County are very patriotic and proud of their country, the United States. In the words of Henry Clay Gorrell on behalf of the Guilford Grays during the crowing of the May queen at Edgeworth Female Seminary in 1860, "And we would have you remember that we are all in favor of union—union of States, union of hearts, union of hands, union now and forever, one and inseparable."[190]

Notes

Abbreviations:
OR: *The War of the Rebellion: A Compilation of the Official Records of the Union and Confederate Armies.*

Depending on the year of publication, the Greensboro Patriot *alternately was spelled* Greensborough Patriot. *All attempts have been made to use the correct spelling for the date of each article in individual citations.*

Acknowledgements

1. *Greensborough Patriot*, April 6, 1865.

Introduction

2. *Greensboro Patriot*, March 23, 1866.
3. Branson, *North Carolina Business Directory*.
4. Ibid.
5. *Greensborough Patriot*, March 27, 1862.
6. Ibid., July 23, 1862.

CHAPTER 1

7. *Greensborough Patriot*, May 18, 1860.
8. Ibid.
9. "The Disciple of Friends," http://www.docsouth.unc.edu/nc/friends1823/friends.html.
10. Ibid.

CHAPTER 2

11. Gilmer, "State of the Union."
12. Ibid.
13. Konklc, *John Motley Morehead*, 391.
14. Cole, *Seven Decades*, 37.
15. Ibid.
16. Sloan, *Reminiscences of Guilford Grays*, 22.
17. *Greensborough Patriot Semi-Weekly*, June 28, 1861.
18. Tinsley, "First Memorial Association Formed Here."

CHAPTER 3

19. OR: series 4, volume 1, 192.
20. *Greensborough Patriot*, May 8, 1862.
21. *Wilmington (NC) Journal*, February 17, 1862.
22. OR: series 1, volume 19, part 2, 681.
23. Ibid., series 4, volume 2, 176.
24. *Greensborough Patriot*, February 20, 1862.
25. Ibid., February 6, 1862.
26. Ibid., April 10, 1862.
27. Ibid.
28. Ibid., February 13, 1862.
29. Sloan, *Reminiscences of Guilford Grays*, 37.
30. Adams's grave epitaph at Green Hill Cemetery.
31. Brown and Coffey, *North Carolina Troops*, 11:103.

CHAPTER 4

32. *Greensborough Patriot*, February 5, 1863.
33. Ibid., August 1863.
34. Ibid., January 8, 1863.
35. Ibid., November 26, 1863.
36. Ibid., April 16, 1863.
37. Ibid.
38. Ibid.
39. Smith and Wilson, *North Carolina Women*.
40. Ibid.
41. *Greensborough Patriot*, August 27, 1862.
42. Ibid.
43. Ibid., July 23, 1863.
44. Ibid., September 3, 1863.
45. Ibid., July 23, 1863.
46. Ibid., September 10, 1863.
47. Ibid.
48. Ibid., February 18, 1864.
49. Ibid., September 3, 1863.
50. Ibid., August 27, 1863.
51. Ibid., November 13, 1863.
52. Ibid., November 5, 1863.
53. Ibid., November 19, 1863.
54. Ibid., July 13, 1863.

CHAPTER 5

55. *Greensboro Patriot*, January 21, 1864.
56. Ibid., February 4, 1864.
57. Ibid.
58. Ibid., February 18, 1864.
59. Ibid.
60. Ibid., February 11, 1864.
61. Ibid.
62. Ibid.
63. Ibid.

64. *Raleigh, North Carolina Standard—Semi-Weekly Standard*, February 9, 1864.
65. *Greensborough Patriot*, January 14, 1864.
66. Ibid., March 31, 1864.
67. Ibid., April 21, 1864.
68. Wyche, *History of Nursing*, 18–19.
69. *Greensborough Patriot*, March 1, 1864.
70. Ibid., March 24, 1864.
71. Ibid., May 5, 1864.
72. OR: series 4, volume 2, 394.
73. *Greensborough Patriot*, March 3, 1864.
74. Ibid.
75. Ibid., September 29, 1864.
76. Ibid., May 12, 1864.
77. Brown and Coffey, *North Carolina Troops*, 18:296, 309, 314.
78. Ibid., June 23, 1864.
79. Ibid., May 12, 1864.
80. Ibid., September 1864.
81. Smith, "Women of Greensboro."
82. *Greensborough Patriot*, July 8, 1864.
83. Sloan, *Reminiscences of Guilford Grays*, 91.
84. Ibid., 95.
85. *Greensborough Patriot*, June 23, 1864.
86. Ibid.
87. Ibid., August 11, 1864.
88. Sloan, *Reminiscences of Guilford Grays*, 102–4.
89. *Greensboro Patriot*, September 18, 1864.
90. Ibid., September 29, 1864.
91. OR: series 1, volume 39, part 2, 462.
92. *Greensborough Patriot*, December 1, 1864.
93. Brown and Coffey, *North Carolina Troops*, 1:134.
94. *Charlotte (NC) Western Democrat*, November 29, 1864.
95. *Greensborough Patriot*, November 3, 1864.
96. Sloan, *Reminiscences of Guilford Grays*, 130.
97. *Greensborough Patriot*, November 17, 1864.
98. OR: series 1, volume 42, part 3, 1,348.

CHAPTER 6

99. *Greensborough Patriot*, January 26, 1865.
100. Ibid.
101. OR: series 1, volume 46, part 2, 1,221.
102. *Greensborough Patriot*, February 9, 1865.
103. Ibid.
104. Smith, "Women of Greensboro."
105. Ibid.
106. *Greensborough Patriot*, April 6, 1865.
107. OR: series 1, volume 47, part 3, 725–6.
108. Ibid.
109. Athos, "Greensboro in April, 1865," *Greensboro Patriot*, March 23, 1866.
110. Arnett, *Confederate Guns*, 149.
111. Trelease, *North Carolina Railroad*, 192.
112. OR: series 1, volume 47, part 3, 789.
113. Sutherland, "Wood, John Taylor."
114. Arnett, *Confederate Guns*, 36.
115. Alfriend, *Life of Jefferson Davis*, 625–26.
116. OR: series 1, volume 47, part 3, 787.
117. Smith, "Women of Greensboro."
118. OR: series 1, volume 47, part 3, 804.
119. Ibid., 805.
120. Ibid., 809.
121. Ibid., 810.
122. Ibid., 811.
123. Ibid.
124. Ibid., 815.
125. Ibid., volume 53, 419.
126. Stockard, *History of Guilford County*, 67.
127. OR: series 1, volume 38, part 1, 49.
128. Ibid., volume 47, part 3, 843.
129. Ibid., 856.
130. Athos, "Greensboro in April, 1865," *Greensboro Patriot*, March 23, 1866.
131. Ibid.
132. Smith, "Women of Greensboro."
133. Walker, "Federals in Greensboro."
134. Jordan and Manning, *Women of Guilford County*, 57.
135. OR: series 1, volume 47, part 3, 450.

136. *Greensboro Patriot*, March 16, 1866.
137. Powell, "Dictionary of North Carolina Biography."
138. OR: series 1, volume 47, part 1, 185.
139. Ibid., 185–86.
140. *Greensborough Patriot*, July 22, 1865.

CHAPTER 7

141. *Greensboro Patriot*, April 6, 1866.
142. Ibid., May 11, 1866.
143. Craig, "Venture in Home Ownership."
144. Ibid.
145. Arnett, *Confederate Guns*.
146. Diane Lamb, "African Americans in Guilford County," http://nrtimelines.wikifoundry.com/page/African+Americans+in+Guilford+County (accessed January 22, 2015).
147. Sloan, *Reminiscences of Guilford Grays*, 30.
148. Union Cemetery grave monument.
149. Simpson, *First Presbyterian Church*.
150. Ibid., 12.
151. Jaime Huaman, "Greensboro Four: David Richmond, Franklin, McCain, Ezell Blair Jr. (Jibreel Khazan), Joe McNeil," http://ncpedia.org/history/20th-Century/greensboro-four.

CHAPTER 8

152. Tinsley, "First Memorial Association."
153. Ibid.
154. *Greensboro Patriot*, May 11, 1866.
155. Letter from S.C. Caldwell to Bettie Caldwell dated April 7, 1909 (clipping file, Greensboro Public Library).
156. *Greensboro Patriot*, May 12, 1870.
157. Ibid.
158. Ibid.
159. Ibid.

160. Ibid., May 11, 1871.
161. Ibid., May 9, 1872; Tinsley.
162. *Greensboro (NC) New North State*, May 14, 1873.
163. *Greensboro Patriot*, May 17, 1876.
164. Ibid., July 5, 1876.
165. Ibid.
166. Ibid., May 17, 1876.
167. *Greensboro Daily News*, May 7, 1879.
168. *Greensboro Patriot*, February 14, 1884; *Greensboro North State*, February 14, 1884, and February 21, 1884.
169. *North State Newspaper*, April 26, 1888.
170. Inscription dedication, November 17, 2007.
171. *Greensboro Patriot*, May 10, 1893.
172. Ibid., July 5, 1899.
173. *Greensboro (NC) News and Observer*, June 25, 1899.
174. Ibid., July 5, 1899.
175. MacKethan, *Chapter Histories*, 56–58.
176. *Greensboro Patriot*, May 15, 1901.
177. Ibid., May 13, 1915.
178. *Norwich Bulletin*, June 11, 1914.
179. *Greensboro Daily News*, May 11, 1916.
180. Ibid., May 11, 1930.
181. Ibid.
182. Ibid.
183. Arnett, *Confederate Guns*, 320.
184. *Daily Record*, May 9, 1940.
185. Inscription dedication, November 17, 2007.
186. Author's recollection.
187. The Confederate Officers of North Carolina Society, Military Order of Stars and Bars, http://www.mosbnc.org.

CONCLUSION

188. Phone interview and letters from Mary Lowrey Armstrong Stewart.
189. *Greensborough Patriot*, February 11, 1864.
190. Ibid., May 18, 1860.

Bibliography

Books

Albright, James W., comp. *Greensboro 1808–1904: Facts Figures, Traditions, and Reminiscences*. Reprint, Salem, MA: Higginson Book Co., 1904.

Arnett, Ethel Stephens. *Confederate Guns Were Stacked Greensboro North Carolina.* Greensboro, NC: Piedmont Press, 1965.

———. *Greensboro North Carolina: The County Seat of Guilford.* Chapel Hill: University of North Carolina Press, 1955.

Brown, Mathew M., and Michael W. Coffey, eds. *North Carolina Troops, 1861–1865; a Roster.* Vols. 16–19. Raleigh, NC: State Department of Archives and History, 2009–2013.

Caldwell, Bettie D. *Founders and Builders of Greensboro, 1808–1908*. Greensboro, NC: Joseph J. Stone & Co., 1925.

Clark, Walter, ed. *Histories of the Several Regiments and Battalions from North Carolina in the Great War 1861–1865, Written by Members of Their Respective Commands.* 5 vols. Wilmington, NC: Broadfoot Publishing Co., 1996.

Cole, James Reid. *Seven Decades of My Life*. Dallas, TX: John F. Worley Printing Co., 1913.

Foley, Bradley, and Adrian L. Whicker. *The Civil War Ends, Greensboro, April 1865.* Greensboro, NC: Guilford County Genealogical Society, 2008.

Hobbs, Mary Mendenhall. *Civil War and Reconstruction Through the Eyes of Mary Mendenhall Hobbs.* Reprint, Winston-Salem, NC: Mary Mendenhall Hobbs Group of the North Carolina Friends Historical Society, 2012.

Jordan, Paula, and Kathy W. Manning, researcher. *Women of Guilford County, North Carolina.* Greensboro, NC: Greensboro Printing Company, 1979.

Jorden, Weymoth T., Jr., and Louis H. Manarin, comp. *North Carolina Troops, 1861–1865; A Roster.* Vols. 1–15. Raleigh, NC: State Department of Archives and History, 1966.

MacKethan, Edwin R. *Chapter Histories North Carolina Division United Daughters of the Confederacy 1897–1947.* United States: North Carolina Division United Daughters of the Confederacy, 1947/2007.

Moore, Carol. *Greensboro's Confederate Soldiers.* Charleston, SC: Arcadia Publishing, 2008.

———. *Greensboro's First Presbyterian Church Cemetery.* Charleston, SC: Arcadia Publishing, 2006.

Simpson, John Wells. *History of the First Presbyterian Church of Greensboro.* Greensboro, NC, 1945.

Sloan, John A. *Reminiscences of Guilford Grays, Co. B, 27th NC Regiment.* Washington, D.C.: R.O. Polkinhorn, Printer, 1883.

Smith, Margaret Supplee, and Emily Herring Wilson. *North Carolina Women: Making History.* Chapel Hill: University of North Carolina Press, 1999.

Spencer, Cornelia Phillips. *The Last Ninety Days of the War in North Carolina.* Wilmington, NC: Broadfoot Publishing Co., 1993.

Stockard, Sallie W. *The History of Guilford County, N.C.* Knoxville, TN: Gaut-Ogden Co., 1902.

Trealease, Allen W. *The North Carolina Railroad, 1849–1871, and the Modernization of North Carolina.* Chapel Hill: University of North Carolina Press, 1991.

PAMPHLETS

Gilmer, John Adams. "State of the Union: speech of Hon. John A. Gilmer, of North Carolina: delivered in the House of Representatives, January 26, 1861." Washington, D.C.: H. Polkinhorn, printer, 1861.

Jones, Nellie Rowe. "Guilford Under the Stars and Bars." Clipping file, Greensboro Public Library, Greensboro, NC.

Smith, Mary Watson. "Women of Greensboro, N.C. 1861–1865." A paper by Mrs. J. Henry Smith read at a meeting of the United Daughters of the Confederacy at Greensboro. Little Rock, AK: Democrat P.&L. Co., 1919.

ARTICLES

"Athos." "Greensboro in 1865." *Greensboro Patriot*, March 23, 1866.

Craig, Nell. "Venture in Home-Ownership by Means of Modest and Long-Term Payments Started After Civil War." *Greensboro Daily News*, June 1, 1941.

Greensboro Daily News. "Eighteen Old Confederates Assemble in Annual Meeting." May 11, 1930.

Greensborough Patriot. "The Coronation." May 18, 1860.

Morton, Mrs. Frank P. "Early Memorial Days in City Remembered," May 13, 1944. Clipping file, Greensboro Public Library.

Tinsley, Annette Sloan. "First Memorial Association Formed Here May 11, 1866, Honoring Confederate Dead." *Greensboro Daily News*. Clipping file, Greensboro Public Library.

———. "Greensboro's First Memorial Day." *Greensboro Daily Record*, May 13, 1944.

Walker, Letitia Morehead. "The Federals in Greensboro." *Charlotte Observer*, January 11, 1901.

NEWSPAPERS

Greensboro (NC) Daily News

Greensboro/Greensborough (NC) Patriot

Greensboro (NC) New North State

Greensboro (NC) News and Observer

Greensboro (NC) North State

Greensborough (NC) Patriot Semi-Weekly

Raleigh (NC) North Carolina Standard—Semi-Weekly Standard.

Wilmington (NC) Journal

INTERNET SOURCES

Alfriend, Frank H. *The Life of Jefferson Davis.* San Francisco, California: Cincinnati, OH: Claxton Publishing House, 1868. Project Gutenberg. http://www.gutenberg.org/files/43329/43329- h/43329-h.htm (accessed October 16, 2014).

Betts, Alexander D. "Experiences of a Confederate Chaplain." *Documenting the American South.* docsouth.unc.edu (accessed September 2, 2014).

Branson, Levi. *Branson & Farrar's North Carolina Business Directory Containing Facts, Figures, Names and Locations*. Electronic edition. http://docsouth.unc.edu/nc/branson/branson.html (accessed September 3, 2014).

Charlotte (NC) Western Democrat, November 29, 1864. Chronicling America: Historic American Newspapers. http://chroniclingamerica.loc.gov/lccn/sn84020712/1864-11-29/ed-1/seq-1/ (accessed November 15, 2015).

Chronicling America: Historic American Newspapers. http://chroniclingamerica.loc.gov/ (accessed 2014).

Cornell University Library. "Making of America Digital Collection." http://ebooks.library.cornell.edu/m/moa/permissions.html (accessed 2014).

Cox, Jacob Dolson Cox. *Military Reminiscences of the Civil War V2*. Project Gutenberg EBook, 2004. http://www.gutenberg.org/files/6962/6962-h/6962-h.htm (accessed 2014).

Documenting the American South. docsouth.unc.edu (accessed 2014).

Gilmer, John. "State of the Union: Speech of Hon. John A. Gilmer, of North Carolina: Delivered in the House of Representatives, January 26, 1861." Internet Archive. http://archive.org/stream/stateofunionspee00gilm/stateofunionspee00gilm_djvu.txt (accessed November 12, 2014).

Harper's Weekly. http://quod.lib.umich.edu/h/harpersweeklyic/x-1865/18650340 (accessed November 15, 2014).

———. http://quod.lib.umich.edu/h/harpersweeklyic/x-1865/18650332 (accessed November 15, 2014).

Hilty, Hiram H. *Toward Freedom for All North Carolina Quakers and Slavery*. Internet Archive. https://archive.org/stream/towardfreedomfor00hilt/towardfreedomfor00hilt_djvu.txt (accessed November 16, 2014).

Konkle, Burton Alva. *John Motley Morehead and the Development of North Carolina 1796–1866*. Philadelphia, PA: William J. Campbell, 1922. https://archive.org/stream/johnmotleymorehe00konk#page/n7/mode/2up (accessed November 17, 2014).

Library of Congress. http://www.loc.gov (accessed 2014).

North Carolina Civil War Sesquicentennial. http://www.nccivilwar150.com/timeline/1865.htm (accessed October 12, 2014).

Norwich (CT) Bulletin, June 11, 1914. Chronicling America: Historic American Newspapers. http://chroniclingamerica.loc.gov/lccn/sn82014086/1914-06-11/ed-1/seq-10 (accessed October 5, 2014).

Powell, William S., ed. Dictionary of North Carolina Biography. http://www.docsouth.unc.edu/church/tourgee/bio.html (accessed January 22, 2015).

Stockard, Sallie W. *The History of Guilford County, 1902*. Internet Archive. archive.org/details/historyofguilford00stoc (accessed October 12, 2014).

Sutherland, David A. "Wood, John Taylor." In *Dictionary of Canadian Biography*, vol. 13, University of Toronto/Université Laval, 2003–. http://www.biographi.ca/en/bio/wood_john_taylor_13E.html (accessed September 19, 2014).

United Daughters of the Confederacy. Minutes of the tenth annual convention of the United Daughters of the Confederacy: [serial] North Carolina Division (1899). Internet Archives. http://www.archive.org/details/minutesofannualc1909unit and https://archive.org/details/minutesofannu1917unit (accessed November 7, 2014).

United States War Department. *The War of the Rebellion: A Compilation of the Official Records of the Union and Confederate Armies*. Washington, D.C.: Government Printing Office, various years. http://ebooks.library.cornell.edu/m/moawar/waro.html (accessed January 22, 2015).

University of Michigan Library Digital Collections. *Harper's Weekly*. http://quod.lib.umich.edu/h/harpersweeklyic/x-1865/18650332 and http://quod.lib.umich.edu/h/harpersweeklyic/x-1865/18650340 (accessed October 27, 2014).

Wikipedia. "Guilford County, North Carolina." http://en.wikipedia.org/wiki/Guilford_County,_North_Carolina (accessed October 12, 2014).

Wyche, Mary Lewis. *The History of Nursing in North Carolina*. Chapel Hill: University of North Carolina, 1938. http://www.scribd.com/doc/63816424/The-History-of-Nursing-in-North-Carolina (accessed December 3, 2014).

LOCATIONS VISITED

Blandwood, Greensboro, NC.
Gibsonville, NC.
Green Hill Cemetery, Greensboro, NC.
Greensboro Historical Museum, Greensboro, NC.
Greensboro Public Library, Greensboro, NC.
High Point Museum, High Point, NC.
Jamestown, NC.
McLeansville, NC.
Oak Ridge, NC.
Oakwood Municipal Cemetery, High Point, NC.
Summerfield, NC.
Union Cemetery, Greensboro, NC.

Index

F

G

H

J

L

About the Author

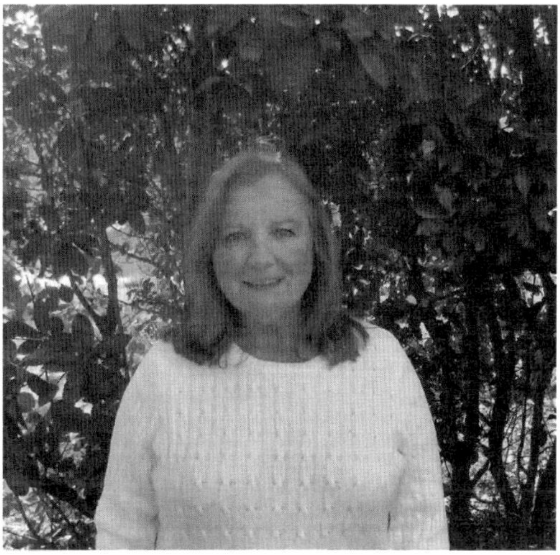

Carol Moore—a native of Jefferson County, Kentucky, and a resident of Guilford County, North Carolina—has an avid interest in the history of the United States, particularly Southern history. Her history passion has been lifelong and began with genealogy and family stories told through story and song heard while sitting on her grandparents' cabin porch located in an isolated "holler" on the Cumberland Plateau of the Appalachian Mountains. The isolation of the area instilled in her a passion for nineteenth-century history because she witnessed that lifestyle personally in her youth.

Carol was awarded the Willie Parker Peace History Book Award by the North Carolina Society of Historians for her books *Greensboro's First Presbyterian Church Cemetery* in 2006 and *Greensboro's Confederate Soldiers* in 2008. The United Daughters of the Confederacy presented her with a Jefferson Davis Historical Gold Medal in 2008 for her historical research and publications.

Additionally, the North Carolina Society Order of Confederate Rose awarded Carol the Annabelle Robinson Edgerton Southern History Award in 2009.

In her spare time, Carol reads, gardens, travels and tends to her four-legged kids (who do not realize they are cats and dogs), but her greatest passion is studying nineteenth-century history. One of Carol's core beliefs is that one should give back to the community in which one resides. She fulfills this belief by volunteering in local museums and presenting historic programs to heritage and genealogical organizations.